Marching
to a
Different Drummer

Rediscovering Missions
in an
Age of Affluence and Self-Interest

D1557056

Marching
to a
Different Drummer

Rediscovering Missions
in an
Age of Affluence and Self-Interest

by Jim Raymo

Christian • Literature • Crusade
Fort Washington, Pennsylvania 19034

CHRISTIAN LITERATURE CRUSADE

U.S.A.
P.O. Box 1449, Fort Washington, PA 19034

GREAT BRITAIN
51 The Dean, Alresford, Hants., SO24 9BJ

AUSTRALIA
P.O. Box 91, Pennant Hills, N.S.W. 2120

NEW ZEALAND
10 MacArthur Street, Feilding

ISBN 0-87508-719-1

PRINTED IN THE UNITED STATES OF AMERICA

ACKNOWLEDGEMENTS

The 1993-95 MARC *Missions Handbook* reported a decline in the number of Protestant career missionaries. This decline certainly merits investigation. What you are about to read is a compilation of research and interviews I have had with key mission leaders and other Christian thinkers concerning the factors leading to this decline.

Before I go further, I want to thank those who have helped in the preparation of this book. Among these are my wife Judy, Stewart Dinnen, John Whittle, Elwin Palmer, Marjorie McDermid, Aleta Matthews and Nancy Land—all members of WEC International—who were willing to read the manuscript and suggest areas where gaps existed or where support for my conclusions was inadequate. I want also to thank Stan Guthrie of the Evangelical Information Center for his help in locating resource material. I am very grateful to Dr. Robertson McQuilkin, President Emeritus of Columbia International University, for his continued encouragement concerning the publishing of this manuscript. Thanks to Bob and Betty Jo Ambler for their work in requesting publishing rights for quoted material. For their practical help and skills, I thank Robert Delancy,

Willard Stone and Dick Brodhag of Christian Literature Crusade—the book's publisher.

I want also to express my appreciation for time given for interviews and guidance by Dr. Dieter Kuhl–International Secretary, WEC International; Dr. Harvie Conn–Professor, Westminster Theological Seminary, Philadelphia, Pa.; Dr. James Engel–Professor, Eastern College, St. Davids, Pa.; Dr. John Orme–Executive Director of IFMA; Dr. Ralph Winter–Founder/Director, U.S. Center for World Missions; Dr. Bob Coote–Researcher, Overseas Ministries Study Center; Rev. Paul McKaughan–Executive Director of the EFMA; Dr. Brian Woodford–International Training and Resources Secretary, WEC International; Mr. Patrick Johnstone–International Research Secretary, WEC International; Dr. Helen Roseveare–missionary and author, WEC International; Dr. Thena Ayres–Professor, Regent College, Vancouver, B.C., Canada; Dr. Brian Stelck–President, Carey Theological College, Vancouver, B.C., Canada; Dr. Tom Marks–WEC International; and Dr. John Jackson–Executive Minister, American Baptist Church of the Pacific Southwest.

The missiological counsel and opinions I received from these persons, as well as suggestions about valuable resources concerning the present and future need for career missionaries, were helpful and varied widely.

Some of my expert interviewees believe that the missiological "center of gravity" has moved to the non-Western nations and that the West should *recognize this* and be prepared to carry different responsibilities—to concentrate particularly on such areas as finance, strategy, mentoring and training. Others strongly assert the need for the West and non-West to continue, *as partners*, the pioneering task of planting churches among the remaining unreached peoples of the world. The conclusions reached in this investigation are my own, and only specific quotations come from any of the persons listed above.

All Scripture quotations are from the *New International Version* (NIV) of the Bible unless otherwise noted.

DEDICATION

I gratefully dedicate this book to my wife Judy, whose quiet, faithful support has been a blessing these twenty years of marriage; and to my parents, Mary and Gordon, whose gift for making friends out of strangers has been both a helpful model and an encouraging example.

CONTENTS

FOREWORD

When I first met Jim Raymo—and Judy, his wife-to-be—they were doing evangelism and discipleship in London with a group of University of Minnesota students, based in an unused warehouse on the grounds of WEC International, west of the city. I was immediately struck by his gentleness. He cared deeply for each student's personal welfare and spiritual walk. They had transformed the empty warehouse into dormitories, a sitting-room, dining and kitchen areas, and the whole place was permeated with the love of our Lord Jesus Christ. Jim led the team with firmness, and yet with kindliness and keen perception of individual needs. I was impressed—and looked forward to being invited to share the Word of God with these young people at their daily devotional meeting. Their lives were busy with creative work, traveling to and from London, selling handmade gift items and seeking to share Jesus with those who stopped to look at their wares: yet always, this time for prayer and Bible study was jealously guarded as *the* most important point in the day.

Through the following years, from pastoring in Minneapolis to training in WEC International, Pennsylvania; from teaching at the WEC Missionary College in Tasmania to shepherding candidates for full-time cross-cultural missionary service throughout the world in the ranks of WEC, Jim and Judy have never lost their vision that the most important ingredient in the training of missionary recruits is the *spiritual* one. However important a knowledge of cultural anthropology and the intricacies of modern communications may be, these will never—*must* never—displace, let alone replace, the personal light of holiness from close daily relationship with our Lord Jesus Christ. In this late twentieth century 1 Corinthians 13:1 might well be paraphrased: "If I know all there is to know of computerized and electronic communications, and if I understand with ever-increasing clarity the particular needs of every unreached ethnic group in the world, *but have no personal walk with the Lord Jesus Christ, and am not filled to overflowing with His love and grace,* then I am *useless* in the task of winning men and women to put their trust in Him."

Marching to a Different Drummer communicates Jim's conviction that the urgent task of presenting the Word of Reconciliation to every ethnic group in the world today—in a *meaningful* way that makes possible a positive response—demands the active participation of *every* Christian throughout the world. This is no longer the task of the "Westerner" to the rest, nor has it become the task of the "Rest" to the west: it *must*, rather, be the task of *all* the Church to *all* the unreached. Equally, the task will not be achieved by highly advanced state-of-the-art technology—even if backed up by huge financial donations—without humble believers from one group "going and living amongst" others. This "going and living" also demands a foundation of self-sacrifice, burning faith, true holiness, and a belief in the possibility of universal *fellowship* with believers of other cultures. The would-be missionary must accept our Lord's invitation to "deny self, take up the cross and follow Me" (Luke 9:23).

Adopting the culture and customs of the adopted people will certainly involve being immersed in the local language, until one can pray (and joke!) in it without fear or hesitation. It demands a willingness to lay aside one's own cultural background and seek to become identified with those to whom one goes, living as nearly as possible like them in all but that which is opposed to Christianity. A century ago, Robert Murray M'Cheyne said: "My congregation's greatest need is my personal holiness"—that is, my *preaching* but not *living* in accordance with the gospel is worthless for winning converts! Each missionary's personal lifestyle must reflect and be in accord with the words of the Good News—for we *are* the message. "Your actions speak so loudly that I cannot hear your words" must never be true in a negative sense of God's ambassadors. And no amount of hi-tech training can ever replace the need of a humble walk with Jesus.

And *this* is what I have learned to love and respect in Jim and Judy! They reflect Jesus. To know them, to be with them even briefly, is to have been in the presence of our Master, and to have been given a hunger to know Him more fully. *I believe this book has been born out of their love for HIM* and, through Him, for their fellow-men.

Helen Roseveare

During the 1950s and '60s, Helen Roseveare
served with WEC as a missionary doctor in
the Belgian Congo, now Zaire, and founded
a medical school to train African doctors
which continues today. She is the author of
numerous books, including *Give Me This
Mountain*, *Living Sacrifice*, and *Living Holiness*.

INTRODUCTION

My personal background includes twenty-one years of ministry as a missionary: thirteen years of service with Christian Corps, a tentmaking mission organization previously based in Minneapolis, Minnesota, and now nine years with WEC International (Worldwide Evangelization for Christ), an international evangelistic and church-planting agency. I have worked in evangelism and discipleship, done "tentmaking" as an import/export manager, supervised missionary training and preparation, and held various administrative positions.

I first encountered missions and missionaries in Vietnam, as a 1st Lieutenant with the Combat Engineers. Having met Christ only one year previously, while serving with the U.S. Army in Germany, I knew nothing of the work of missions until I met some Christian and Missionary Alliance (C&MA) missionaries doing church planting, medical work, and operating orphanages near Danang in South Vietnam. I remember still how my visits to the missionaries and a particular national pastor and his church were like leaving the war and entering a "colony of heaven." My positive impression of mission work *grew* as I considered the courage evidenced by those missionaries as they lived and ministered in that dangerous, militarily insecure area.

As a result of that encounter and others since, I hold a high view of missions and missionaries to this day.

In my research, I have attempted to address a serious concern recently expressed by Rev. William Waldrop, then Executive Director of one of the most forward-thinking parachurch organizations in North America, ACMC (Advancing Churches in Missions Commitment). He indicated that *if present trends in the American church continue, the whole future regarding career missionaries from the United States is in serious trouble.* (Historically, the term "career missionaries" has referred to those who make missionary service their lifelong occupation; however, to distinguish between short-term and long-term service, in the 1993-95 *Mission Handbook* a career missionary is now defined as one who has spent at least four years in mission service.)

The Fall 1993 edition of *Moody Monthly* featured the topic, "The Shrinking Missionary Force." Discussed therein were issues relating to the decline in career missionary applicants which many long-term agencies are currently experiencing. This decline has also been reported and summarized in the 1993-95 MARC *Mission Handbook* (MARC denotes Missions Advanced Research and Communication Center, a division of World Vision International). *World Pulse,* a newsletter providing information on events affecting the world of missions, summarizes the decline reported in the *Mission Handbook* as follows: "A new chapter in missions history of the North American Protestant church is being written. *For the first time in five decades, the reported number of people from the United States who are overseas missionaries has fallen, from 50,500 in 1988 to 41,142 in 1992."* [1]

Issues that appear to contribute to this decline, and which merit investigation, include the impact on missions of the orientation and philosophy of the "baby boomer" and "baby buster" generations, the tendency of North American churches to promote short-term mission options, and various questions relating to finances and promotion. For instance, according to a survey of Christian "baby boomers" by Dr. James F. Engel and Jerry D. Jones, reported in *Baby Boomers and the Future of World Missions,* over 75 percent of those questioned felt that the need today for overseas missionaries is *not* greater than for people to minister here in the U.S.A. [2] Only *10 percent* felt that spreading the gospel overseas is a high priority! For most North Americans, "There is a higher interest in domestic causes than in world outreach."[3]

As I have worked on the recruiting and candidate training end of missions for a number of years, I have personally observed this decline. As I will continue to serve in this area, I want to deepen my understanding of the trends and help formulate strategies that might increase interest and involvement among North American Christians in *career missionary service.*

In February of 1995 I had a conversation with Patrick Johnstone, author of *Operation World.* He spoke of 2,500 remaining distinct unreached ethno-linguistic peoples.* While considering the task and workers

---

* See page 18.

needed to pioneer church planting among these remaining unreached peoples, Mr. Johnstone expressed
a concern that most Westerners who offer themselves
for missions do so by offering a specific technical skill
or service. Few come out with a desire to reach men
and women for Jesus Christ in a *pioneering* setting. This
may represent a pendulum swing from the period of
time when it was perceived that all who entered missions work went only to the jungles. The clarion call
has gone out and *been heard* for "support personnel."
The call *now* is for pioneers, evangelists and church
planters, some to the jungles but many to the urban
centers of the world.

In my discussion with Patrick, he affirmed the
need for a new generation of career missionaries who
bring with them:
— a passion for evangelistic, church-planting
ministry.
— missiological knowledge and skills.
— appreciation of the need for cross-cultural
sensitivity.
— awareness of and appreciation for national
church/mission partnership.
— a commitment level equaling that of 19th century missionaries, who traveled overseas resolved to
pay the ultimate price, if necessary, to see the church
planted in new areas.

---

* The numbers of remaining unreached peoples seems to be a moving target. Patrick suggests 2,500, and his rationale for that is provided
in part in Chapter Ten. More information can be attained from Patrick
Johnstone, WEC International, Bulstrode, Gerrards Cross, Bucks, Eng-
land SL9 8SZ.

— a flexible commitment to a region of the world or group of peoples, with a willingness to move and adjust in accord with changing political situations.

The results of research and interviews concerning the decline in career missionary applicants have been interpreted and explained by the following ideologies and patterns of North American church life:

1. The triumph of a self-centered lifestyle and philosophy among American Christians resulting in obsession with personal and local needs. This includes the replacement of prayer and intercession with sharing, fellowship, counseling and recovery groups.

2. A theological shift away from serious convictions about the final judgment and hell.

3. A perceived threat to family life overseas, including separation from children for education. This includes the concern for safety amidst global reports of tribal conflicts, military takeovers, terrorism and Christian martyrdom.

4. Fear or shame regarding raising missionary support.

5. Prospective applicants' existing debts and financial commitments.

6. The impression that technology, tentmakers and short-term workers are adequate substitutes for career missionaries.

7. A perceived shift in the responsibility for world evangelization to nations outside North America.

I intend to scrutinize the above list of sentiments, ideologies and current trends which have had the effect of undermining missions (namely, self-centeredness, relativism, "family first" philosophy, and economic affluence) and to analyze the proposed or inferred *substitutes* for career missions (that is, short-term volunteers, tentmaking, non-Western missionaries replacing Western missionaries). The issues will not be dealt with exhaustively or in an encyclopedic manner, but with the purpose of brief exposure and consideration. My purpose is not primarily that of an *analyst* of trends but rather a *catalyst* for global evangelism and church planting.

Undoubtedly, the reason for the decline in North American career missionaries is a complex mixture of those elements stated above. Other possibly less-influential factors include the perception of past mission mistakes such as *colonialism* and the question of whether North Americans are really *needed* or *wanted* in light of ever-changing political situations abroad. One difficult-to-track issue is whether mission boards are themselves becoming more *selective* in terms of who is acceptable for a given field. Certainly the mission *I* work with has taken pains to enhance its candidate selection process, and fields are pleading for *quality* over *quantity* in the workers sent to the field.

Dr. David Hesselgrave, Professor Emeritus of Missions at Trinity Evangelical Divinity School and Executive Director of the Evangelical Missiological Society, believes that statistics reveal several new trends. In an April 1993 article of *World Pulse* he says that these trends include replacement of long-termers with short-termers, retirement of many post-World War II missionaries, the rising cost of support for their successors, and the increasing number of local churches that bypass mission agencies, follow their own agendas, and send their own people. The implication for this *last* category is that those numbers would not appear in any statistical analysis.

It is not my intent to suggest that every Christian should minister cross-culturally or that every missionary will do career service overseas. Rather, under God's sovereign leadership the question we need to ask is *where does each of us fit in God's missionary agenda for the world,* for which every Christian has some responsibility. Tentmakers and short-termers are filling critical gaps in mission outreach. But some who perceive these as *substitutes* for career missionary work need to reconsider. Are long-term results the product of short-term efforts?

Jim Reapsome writes of Hudson Taylor "who criss-crossed the United States and Canada seeking prayers and volunteers for China's lost millions. . . . He compared China's daily death toll to the deluge of water pouring over Niagara Falls. His graphic picture gripped many Christians, motivating them to take the gospel to China."[4] And the rest is history. This "career commitment" made by large numbers of volunteers established the church throughout China's inland territories. Many missionaries died. But today a thriving church exists in China. It is my premise that such pioneers are still needed in this day so that "this gospel of the kingdom will be preached in the whole world as a testimony to all nations, and then the end will come." (Matthew 24:14)

Marching to a Different Drummer

Mission history is replete with examples of men

and women who, in the light of discovering the privilege of serving God cross-culturally and in direct obedience to His command to go, have left their home countries.

Consider, for example, the life and death of Dr. Paul Carlson, noted in Dr. James Dobson's book *When God Doesn't Make Sense.* In 1961 he joined a relief agency to serve as a medical missionary in the Belgian Congo. It was only a six-month commitment, but what he saw there changed his life. When he returned to his thriving medical practice in Redondo Beach, California, he could not forget the hopeless African people. He told a colleague, "If you could only see [the need], you wouldn't be able to swallow your sandwich!" Soon, Dr. Carlson moved his family to Africa and set up a makeshift clinic, operating at times by flashlight and making house calls on his motorbike. His salary dropped to $3230 a year, but money didn't matter. *He was marching to a different drummer.* Two years later, however, Dr. Carlson became a pawn in a bloody confrontation between rival revolutionary factions in the Belgian Congo. He was among a small band of Americans who were held captive near the battle zone. They had one fleeting opportunity to escape by scaling a wall and dropping to safety on the other side. Dr. Carlson reached the top of the barrier and was a split second from freedom when a burst of bullets tore through his body.[5]

This physician left home, safety, and a lucrative career to serve. His commitment cost him his life. And the costly march *continues.*

CHAPTER ONE

Statistical Interpretation of the MARC *Mission Handbook* (1993-95)

"... the numerical growth rate of career missionaries over the last twenty-five years has failed to keep pace with the population growth rate in North America, let alone with the growth rates in regions of the globe least exposed to the Gospel."— Dr. Bob Coote, *International Bulletin of Missionary Research*, January 1995

"For the first time in five decades, the reported number of people from the United States who are overseas missionaries has fallen, from 50,500 in 1988 to 41,142 in 1992."—Stan Guthrie, *World Pulse,* April 1993; taken from statistics in the 1993-95 *Mission Handbook*

1

Statistics and reports relative to the declining missionary force assault us from all sides, causing alarm signals to go off among those committed to the world missions movement:

—The Interdenominational Foreign Missions Association reports a shrinking trend in the number of IFMA short-term and career missionaries: from an all-time high of 9170 in 1989 to 8900 in 1993.

—The Evangelical Fellowship of Missions Agencies reports another drop in missionaries, the third such decline in the last five reporting years.

—Dr. James Engel, in his survey of Christian baby boomers (see pages 38-39 for definition and characteristics), reports that "Only 10 percent agreed that spreading the gospel overseas is a high priority . . . there is higher interest in domestic causes than in world outreach."[1]

—In his study of evangelical collegians and seminarians, author James Hunter (*Evangelicalism in the Coming Generation*) supports these findings that world evangelization is becoming a reduced priority, at least among younger baby boomers.

—Doug Christgau writes, "The fact that only 0.5 percent of church spending goes to frontier missions may trouble us greatly, but most of the congregation don't know what frontier missions is all about."[2]

—Facing an estimated shortfall of $5 million in 1995, the Episcopal Church plans to cut off support for its missionaries. "I think it's heartbreaking," says

Tom Prichard, Executive Director of the South American Missionary Society (SAMS), the largest missions agency in the Episcopal Church. "This represents the end of a long, sad decline of the church's commitments to missions. The Episcopal Church supported 480 missionaries as recently as 1965, but that number has plunged to 20."[3]

Statistical Analysis and Interpretation

Though research statistics and analysis are not scintillating to all, it is essential that we examine these surveys which form the basis for concern about declining numbers of career missionaries. Assistance in understanding and interpreting these statistics has been provided by Dr. Bob Coote, who works in the Research and Planning Department of the Overseas Ministries Study Center.

In the January 1995 *International Bulletin of Missionary Research*, Dr. Coote has an article entitled, "Good News, Bad News: North American Protestant Overseas Personnel Statistics in Twenty-five Year Perspective." In this he analyzes the decline over the past 25 years reported in MARC's *Mission Handbook* and reminds us that statistics and quantitative judgments must be understood in light of more significant qualitative issues. The article attempts to deepen our understanding of the decline of the missionary force over a sufficient length of time to provide a sense of trends. Dr. Coote recognizes the difficulty of obtaining total accuracy in so fluid an enterprise as missions, where workers are constantly coming and going. He praises the efforts and results of the editors, John Siewert and

John Kenyon, but questions the veracity of the figures for a number of reasons.[4]

The editors of the *Mission Handbook* (Siewert and Kenyon) themselves express a cautionary note. They warn that compilation and analysis of mission statistics is a very tenuous business. The total number of North American overseas personnel reported includes not only the sum of all the questionnaires returned but some estimates. The *actual number* is undoubtedly different.

Even the definition of long-term and short-term missionaries has changed over the years. Dr. Coote states:

> First of all, in previous years mission agencies were generally invited to have their own definitions of short-term when submitting data to MARC researchers. These definitions vary from agency to agency and even from year to year with the same agency. This is understandable, considering that the individual at the personnel desk who completed the survey questionnaire for 1988 was probably not the one who handled it for 1973 and succeeding years. . . .
>
> In the survey questionnaires returned to MARC, mission agencies reported short-term service that ranged widely, from as little as a week to as long as six years. At the higher end of this range there is overlap with current definitions of career personnel. MARC has developed a new data-collecting scheme and this should yield more precise reporting in the future. However, for the researcher interested in trends over time, it necessitates

making a decision as to which of four categories (2 months to a year, 1-2 years, 2-4 years, over
4 years) are to be considered comparable to the
former category of short-term. The fluctuating re-
interpretation of these figures over the years brings
into question the "bottom line" question of how
large is the decline of career missionaries."[5]

Another factor for interpretation, suggested by
the *Handbook* editors themselves, is an adjustment in
figures from the previous edition. The adjustments are
substantial, and they are downward: nearly 3,000 less
than had been previously reported in the career category. "Taking into account this decrease of 3,000 persons in the career category, the decline from 1988 to
1992 is not 7,000 but 4,000."[6]

Yet another factor to consider in numbering the
mission work force is that there are churches presently
sending out missionaries *independently*. Churches have
been encouraged to identify an unreached people-
group and "adopt" those people for prayer. In some
instances this prayer interest has resulted in a church-
planting team going out to the "adopted" people: for
example the Church Resource Network, based in At-
lanta and working in Croatia. Statistics on such workers are not currently reported as part of the missionary force, though at this point the numbers are so small
the difference in totals would be minor.*

---

*Traditional missionary agencies are happy to see new workers sent
directly from local churches, brimming with enthusiasm and coming
to the field to shoulder part of the unreached-peoples task. However,
experience has shown that frequently these independent teams end up
leaning heavily on the mature agencies and workers for logistical,

Tentmakers

An obvious factor that could distort accuracy in the actual number of overseas missionaries is "high security" workers (many of whom are "tentmakers"). Some missionaries go independently into areas closed to the gospel and do so unannounced, for only by accepting secular employment there will they be granted entrance. Mission agencies may have many such workers but do not publicize them and their whereabouts, or even list them in figures given out to the public—for security reasons.

Attrition

Dr. Ralph Winter, in an interview with this author on the 20th of October 1994, reiterated what David Hesselgrave (see p. 16) reports: Missionaries recruited following World War II and now retiring should be considered an important factor as we consider declining career missionary numbers. Pre-boomers from the WW II era have entered retirement age during the past ten years. The War thrust many young men and women out into the world during the 1940s, and exposure to the world's needs stimulated them to career missionary service and to the founding of missionary sending agencies such as World Vision. As the missionaries of this generation have died or retired, they have *not* been succeeded by an equal number of replacements.

---

leadership, and even pastoral help. Unless the church missionary efforts are led by experienced missionary personnel at home and abroad, they often end up trying to "reinvent the wheel," and frequently must rely heavily on the support of agency missionaries already on the field. Sometimes they flounder and have to return home early.

Another factor is today's accepted notion of "career change." The eleventh edition of the *Mission Handbook* states, "The concept of a missionary career is taking its place alongside other career concepts such as engineering, medicine, or law. North Americans in general move in and out of such careers in overseas ministry, and do so in full expectation that at some point in their life they will change careers or return to their home country."[7]

Further Research Projected

The World Evangelical Fellowship (WEF) has commissioned a research project to identify and verify causes for early home return and attrition of missionaries and to suggest solutions to those problems. This project, called ReMap (Reducing Missionary Attrition Project), focuses on both Western and non-Western missionaries and hopes that as a result of its efforts attrition rates will fall 20 percent by 2005.

Conclusions

Though career missionary statistics require interpretation, we must face the fact that the numbers given in the *Missions Handbook* mean that "the number of men and women sent overseas by denominational and nondenominational mission organizations for what historically has been referred to as 'career' or 'long-term' service has declined. The numbers speak for themselves and are consistent with other apparent changes."[8]

In *Baby Boomers and the Future of World Missions*, Dr. James Engels states that "We cannot escape this conclusion: in spite of some interest in overseas service, only a few are willing to consider a missionary career now."[9]

Though this could be grounds for pessimism in our outlook for the future of missions, we must remember that the work of world evangelization is the Lord's, not ours. It is our privilege but not finally our burden: the Lord has assumed that responsibility. Certainly, God is not wringing His hands in despair over the missions situation, nor has He changed His promise to us: "And I tell you that you are Peter, and on this rock I will build my church, and the gates of Hades will not overcome it." (Matthew 16:18)

CHAPTER TWO

Self-Centered Existence
Versus
World Christian Living

And Jonah stalked
to his shaded seat
and waited for God
to come around
to his way of thinking.
And God is still waiting for a host of Jonahs
in their comfortable houses
to come around
to his way of loving.—Thomas Carlisle

"It's tough to have a significant ministry with people whose top priority is to keep their options open."—Pastor of a "boomer" church

"By concentrating day and night on your feelings, potentials, needs, wants and desires, and by learning to assert them more freely, you do not become a freer, more spontaneous, more creative self: you become a narrower, a more self-centered, more isolated one. You do not grow, you shrink."—Daniel Yankelovich, *New Rules*

2

William J. Bennett, former United States Secretary of Education, has drawn a statistical portrait of the moral, social, and behavioral condition of American society over the past 30 years entitled the *Index of Leading Cultural Indicators*. He reports a decline in American culture and values, and he attributes it to the shifting attitudes and beliefs of the American people. When we trace the basis for this phenomenon we are led to the self-centered mentality of the 1960s: "Do your own thing" and "If it feels good, do it." According to pollster Daniel Yankelovich, "Our society now places less value than before on what we owe others as a matter of moral obligation; less value on sacrifice as a moral good; less value on social conformity, respectability, and observing the rules; and less value on correctness and restraint in matters of physical pleasure and sexuality. Higher value is now placed on things like self-expression, individualism, self-realization and personal choice."[1]

Describing the same trend another way, social scientist James Q. Wilson says, "People, especially young people, have embraced an ethos that values self-expression over self-control."[2]

Attributes of the aggressive '60 counter-culture, though immediately rejected by the mainstream, have quietly yet forcefully made major inroads into our society, changing value systems and people's perceptions of life. The "me" decade is criticized for infatuation with the "unrestrained" self and for producing a "culture of narcissism."[3] But we must face the fact that these "counter-culture" attributes have become widely accepted in American society.

As the 1970s unfolded, many people absorbed the suggestion that they were entitled to greater freedom of choice regarding career, marital arrangements and sexual partners, having children or terminating pregnancies, making commitments or "hanging loose." Happiness and fulfillment became the main goals in life. A perceived "right" to happiness and self-fulfillment has increasingly affected the church: "The spiritual walk of Christian individuals has been retarded by their frequent, if unconscious, support of philosophies and activities contradictory to the Christian perspective. The most obvious failings relate to the acceptance of materialism, hedonism and secular humanism."[4]

A great deal has been written about the evolution of sexual norms, and surveys have presented empirical evidence of the shift in American values. In 1967 a CBS News survey found that 85 percent of parents of college-age youths condemned all premarital sex as morally wrong. Today a majority (63 percent) *condone* it:

> If two people love each other, there's nothing morally wrong with having sexual relations. . . . An expectation of impermanence now seemed normal with a marriage. If the experts of the 1920s counseled women to find fulfillment in an intensive and all-consuming intellectual and sexual relationship with one man, their counterparts in the 1970s told them that fulfillment was not a unitary,

once achieved/always achieved state, that different stages demanded new relationships. In the 1950s as in the 1920s, diamonds were "forever." In the 1970s diamonds were for "now." [5]

Marriage vows are no longer seen as expressing a lifetime commitment. Such underlying assumptions evolved into the '90s credo: *I'm looking out for number one. I have my own life to live. Anything is all right as long as it doesn't hurt someone else.*

Theologian Richard John Neuhaus says the sense of moral absolutes and the consequent shame for transgressing them "faded away not in the moral relativism of the 1960s, as is usually argued, but in the Pollyannaish 1950s when spiritual leaders like Norman Vincent Peale argued that you could have the positive side without the negative, which is philosophically and practically impossible. "After all," adds Neuhaus, "we *should* dislike much about ourselves, because there is much about ourselves that is not only profoundly dislikable but odious. It's not for nothing the Ten Commandments are put in the negative." [6]

The baby-boomer generation had dreams of increasing personal fulfillment and of ever-expanding access to comfort and entertainment, resulting in the greatest sense of *entitlement* (i.e., happiness is my due) in American history. Baby boomers and the succeeding busters tend to own a lot and to expect more as well. Dr. Martin E. P. Seligman, Professor of Psychology at the University of Pennsylvania, writes about boomer/buster expectations:

> Our soaring expectations went beyond consumer goods into non-material matters. We came

to expect our jobs to be more than a way to make a living. Work now needs to be ecologically innocent, comfortable to our dignity, a call to growth and excitement, a meaningful contribution to society—*and* deliver a large paycheck. Married partners once settled for duty, but mates today expect to be ecstatic lovers, intellectual colleagues and partners in tennis and water sports. We even expect our partners to be loving parents, a historical peculiarity to anyone versed in the Victorian child-rearing model. [7]

Cheryl Russell, editor of *American Demographics* magazine, estimates that "baby boomers will work at ten different jobs during their lifetime." [8]

This generation blames its parents for its neuroses; it also accepts that everyone suffers from some sort of dysfunctional relationship. The right book or seminar, though, should provide an instant cure.

Characteristics of the Boomers, Busters and Generation X

Baby boomers and busters are perhaps history's most studied demographic groups. (Generally, baby boomers are said to be those born between 1946 and 1964; baby busters between 1965 and 1981; and Generation X are those born after 1981. Some writers, however, use the latter two labels interchangably, or simply lump them together and call them "twentysomethings.") In terms of expectations and implications for missions, opinions vary. It is difficult to make hardline distinctions about these generations. The following is suggested for consideration.

Viewed sociologically, thirteen characteristics of **baby boomers** have surfaced (as presented in the late '80s by the Wycliffe counseling staff to EFMA/IFMA meetings):

1. Changing attitudes toward leadership and authority, dependence and independence.

2. An attitude of spectatorism, impacted and encouraged by the media.

3. Different styles of facing conflict and different reasons for doing so.

4. Commitment has a different face.

5. An attitude of expectation about fringe benefits and entitlements.

6. Family occupies a different place in the thinking of today's adult.

7. Relationships are stated as being more important but are more difficult to achieve.

8. An ease with technology and a reliance on it to accomplish one's task.

9. Materialism and affluence characterize a young adult's lifestyle and are high values with many.

10. A much more tolerant stance toward issues of morality is exhibited.

11. A new posture on values—away from absolutes and closer to relativism.

12. Gender roles and living arrangements are more varied and relaxed.

13. More behavioral and emotional manifestations in adults of childhood trauma and wounding experiences is a fact of life for many. [9]

Regarding **baby busters,** George Barna sees the following defining points:

1. It's the second-largest generation—numbering 70 million—in our nation's history.

2. They see themselves as individuals who are caring, and very honest about reality. Yet they also have a sense of disillusionment and despair about the future, seeing the world as something not worth inheriting—having been ruined by their predecessors the "boomers."

3. They are driven to community and are a more social, cultural generation.

4. Whereas "boomers" rejected the traditional forms of religion and instead updated them, adding dimensions that reflected their own mores and values and perspectives, "busters" are more likely to reject orthodox Christianity and absolutes outright, substituting various spiritual alternatives (New Age, etc.). [10]

Generation X characteristics include:

1. Dysfunctional families have cast this generation adrift from the traditional anchor of family ties. Relationships between parents and children have lost focus as single parents struggle to survive financially and socially.

2. Emotions play an extremely important role in the lives of "Gen Xers." They want to experience it all—the highs and the lows—and they respond to those who are honest about their own struggles.

3. "Gen X" students find belonging to a group a vital part of their lives. But they won't give the time of day to a group judged to be "exclusive." A whiff of pride, self-centeredness or judgment turns these young adults off!

4. The "heart of the issue" draws this generation away from their daily dichotomy of busyness and

boredom. Reaching out to the inner person catches their attention. [11]

More children and adolescents are being reared in a *parental vacuum*, with television, day-care providers and the schools their main supervisors. There is little expectation that they will learn personal responsibility. Immersed in themselves, often only their *peers* provide any value system and interpretation of life.

In assessing and recruiting for the challenging work of missions, we need to affirm the positive characteristics of both busters and Generation Xers as well as understand that stereotypes of any group of people have weaknesses, given the complex diversity of human personality. The following attributes of busters and Xers may be seen as beneficial for missions:

- comfortableness with technology
- flexibility in gender roles
- quickness to address injustice and engage in change
- concern for the family
- interest in personal growth on the professional, spiritual and emotional level
- openness to multi-ethinicity as a result of multi-ethnic urbanization and multi-cultural universities

Discerning mission personnel should recognize these positive characteristics, while at the same time identifying areas needing maturation in preparation for the stresses of living in a different culture.

A Christian Imperative for All Generations

The Church must be prepared and equipped to challenge each generation to move beyond its hurts, disillusionment, and soured idealism. We may have gone too far in attempting to accommodate the current need to "feel good," thereby producing unhealthy dependencies. An interesting critique from the secular camp expresses the realization that the aggressive search for self-fulfillment fails for lack of scope and vision. *Personal satisfaction is too small a purpose to satisfy us!*

> The concrete implication of this philosophical insight is far-reaching: you do not get in touch with essence of self solely by looking inward. . . . By concentrating day and night on your feelings, potentials, needs, wants and desires, and by learning to assert them more freely, you do not become a freer, more spontaneous, more creative self: you become a narrower, a more self-centered, more isolated one. You do not grow, you shrink. . . . The error of replacing self-denial with a duty-to-self ethic has proven nearly fatal, for nothing has subverted self-fulfillment more thoroughly than self-indulgence. [12]

In contrast, God's plan expressed in Christ is for us to *release* our tight grip on our self-fulfillment agenda and *receive with open hands of faith* His fulfilling plan for our lives. The biblical responses of faith, dependency and trust begin the process of healing. Whenever we place a higher priority on solving our problems than on pursuing God, we are not being fully Christian. Our own comfort, peace, joy and satisfaction are *not* to be our top priorities!

> The loss of appetite for the good things God designed us to enjoy is the most tragic evidence of

the fallen structure. The joy of giving has been re-
placed by the pleasure of getting. The thrill of living as unthreatened people who can continue to
give no matter how we're treated stirs us less than
the chance to protect ourselves against assaults on
our dignity and to affirm our value in the midst of
a demeaning world. And the sheer excitement of
standing fully accepted in the presence of God is
less appealing than straightening out our lives.
Rather than finding God, we prefer to relieve our
terror of life by making money and friends, and
we express our rage at a God who cannot be
trusted by arrogantly trusting ourselves. [13]

When we make it our top priority to become personally healthy and free from low self-esteem and co-
dependencies, the deadly disease of selfishness takes
over. Though it must be conceded that to be *effective in
ministry* a person's emotional problems must be addressed and a measure of healing take place, full healing often may be received in the *midst* of ministering
to others. Hurts should not be trivialized, and we must
be wise about individuals who, because of the sever-
ity of previous trauma, need temporarily or permanently to step back from ministry. *Jesus sent home some
who wanted to be part of His discipleship band.* Christians
must be prepared to lead and not simply jump on the
bandwagon of the latest counseling seminar.

The essentials that guide the Church of Jesus
Christ, founded on His Word, remain unchanged.

The supernatural nature of the church has
enabled it to survive severe persecution, heresy,
poverty, and prosperity. While we may use the
modern disciplines of sociology and management

to be more effective, we dare not reduce the church to a merely human institution. . . . In the commendable effort to be relevant we must be diligent students of people and trends. We must speak the language of our generation and constantly update our ministries if we are to be effective. Because the required effort is great, there may be a temptation to neglect the spiritual. To do so is to tear the heart out of Christian ministry and lower the work of the gospel to something less than supernatural. The uncompromising balance must be maintained, forfeiting neither relevance nor revelation.[14]

The Biblical Answer to Fulfillment

God invites us into union with Himself and His purposes, the remedy for the human situation. *Maturity in this union* provides a basis for cross-cultural ministry. If we refuse communion with God for a lesser alternative, we feel alienation at the most basic level of our being: alienation from the Creator, from other people, and from the world around us. In dissatisfaction of soul, we try to substitute things and people for God, misguidedly seeking happiness. As the songwriter said, we are all "looking for love in all the wrong places," and we conclude that genuine love, consistent peace, true significance and happiness are not really available to humans. The devotional writer Thomas Keating suggests that happiness cannot be found in the programs fashioned in early childhood or later in counseling sessions based on instinctual needs for survival and security, affection, esteem, power and control over as much of life as possible. These programs cannot possibly work in adult life; there is too much about life we cannot control.

One of the many problems with the self-centered view of life is that we tend to see ourselves as wounded victims rather than as sinners before a holy God. Larry Crabb expresses this concern in his book *Finding God*. Two of the most destructive attitudes that pervade our society and churches are:

1. Having my needs fulfilled is the most important thing in life.

2. I am not sure God can be trusted to give me what I really need so I must ultimately fend for myself. [15]

The twentieth-century Westerner wants faith to be easy and painless. We may readily accept the slogan "No pain, no gain" when applied to physical exercise, but we expect Christianity to provide comfort and blessing, not demanding sacrifice. The biblical remedy and only permanently satisfying answer for our need for significance and personal peace is *trust in* and *intimacy with* God. In many ways this cuts across the grain of the influences in our society. George Barna speaks about the litmus test of faith being personal spiritual commitment and states that "It is an undeniable fact of modern life that commitment to a Christian perspective and lifestyle is made difficult by the numerous interests that compete for people's time, energy and intellect, and by the reality that we are limited in the number of substantial obligations we can fulfill." [16]

Knowing Christ, and communing with and obeying Him, was Paul's answer for significance and meaning. "But whatever was to my profit I now consider loss for the sake of Christ. What is more, I consider everything a loss compared to the surpassing greatness of knowing Christ Jesus my Lord." (Philippians 3:7–8)

C.T. Studd, the founder of WEC International, often expressed the importance of not just *knowing* the Lord but also of entering into the fellowship of His *sufferings*. One of C.T.'s statements is now the mission's motto: **"If Jesus Christ be God and died for me, then no sacrifice can be too great for me to make for Him."** Baby-boomer values clash with this attitude. Cynthia Heald of the Navigators writes, "To know God involves a loss of our own agenda. It can require sacrifice, discipline, alertness to those things eternal. More than anything else, it calls for a heart that values Christ above all else." [17]

As Christians we know that ultimately peace, significance and satisfaction are found only in God. God's concerns and agenda can become *ours*. He loves the world enough to die for it, and we (with His spirit transforming us) take on a likeness to our Father in this regard, and *love* His world. His global concern becomes ours in prayer and in helping to build His kingdom.

As previously mentioned, this is not to suggest that every Christian will work overseas, but the entire church *is* given the mandate in Scripture to take on, using current terminology, *a "World Christian" outlook.** In discovering God and His plan for us, we take on His concern for the world. His interests and agenda

*David Bryant of the "Concerts of Prayer" movement describes World Christians as "day-to-day disciples for whom Christ's global cause has become the integrating, overriding priority for all that He is for them. Like disciples should, they actively investigate all that their Master's Great Commision means. Then they act on what they learn." [18]

begin to move in our hearts, liberating us from self-absorption.

Bethany Fellowship Missions states in its promotional material: The question is not "Am I called to missions?" The question is "Where do I fit in God's missionary plan to which every Christian is called?"

A few years ago, the *Los Angeles Times* ran a full-page article about the many psychotherapeutic clinics opening in the area to deal with "yuppie angst." Many young boomers and busters were succeeding spectacularly in their careers and enjoying the perks that come with promotions and success. However, having reached their goals, they were finding themselves increasingly anxious because the achievement was not as satisfying as they expected. What could be worse than to reach the pinnacle of one's aspirations—with the BMW, the beach home, the corner office—and find emptiness and dissatisfaction? Patients were lining up to be counseled about the anxiety (angst) they felt. The counselors' primary recommendation to these depressed yuppies was most interesting: find a charitable, volunteer project and give yourself wholeheartedly to doing good. Forget about your own best interests, invest yourself in others and in worthwhile projects, and you will find peace and fulfillment. Sociologists may refer to this as the "New Volunteerism," but Christians recognize this as discovery and implementation of the truth that satisfaction and meaning in life come through *relationship and service.*

E. Stanley Jones, missionary to India, spoke of his conversion and subsequent launch into God's concern for the world which brought much joy into his life: "I came to Him all unsuspecting. I wanted salvation, and found in taking it I wanted the salvation of the world. I'm taking more and more projects upon myself—world projects. And the more I take on myself, the more I'm taken over by joy, by well-being, by inner excitement, by adventure, by growth, by life."

Many in the evangelical community have detected among today's American Christians a preference for therapy and psychological wholeness above doctrinal correctness. Donald Bloesch questions this in *The Future of Evangelical Christianity*:

> Can we have an integrated personality apart from an integral vision of life? Are deep personal relations with others possible apart from a common faith and commitment? ... Prayer groups and Bible study groups are conducted in such a way that group process techniques tend to impede the free movement of the Holy Spirit. ... The fathers of the faith correctly perceived that the torment of the soul cannot be alleviated by therapeutic and medicinal techniques. "There is death," said Calvin, "even a spiritual death, which cannot be corrected by all the means and nostrums of the world. God has to put forth his hand, and that mightily." [19]

Martyrdom—Embracing His Cross as Ours

On an even more radical level (though a quite ordinary one from the New Testament perspective), we are reminded of martyrs whose least concern was their well-being or esteem—except in the sight of God. George Otis asked the Second Lausanne Congress on

World Evangelization in Manila a set of startling questions: Is our failure to thrive in Muslim countries owing to the absence of martyrs? Can a covert church grow in strength? Does a young church need martyr models? People in many places around the globe understand the words of Jesus with all their radical impact: to choose Christ is to choose *death*, or at least a *high risk* of death. David Barrett estimates that in 1993 about 150,000 Christians throughout the world died as martyrs. He foresees the annual number increasing to 200,000 by the year 2000. [20]

Raymond Lull, called the "first missionary to the Muslims," died a martyr's death. For a time, after some troubling events in evangelistic efforts, he labored among the Muslim community secretly, but—

> At length, weary of seclusion . . . he came forth into the open market and presented himself to the people as the same man whom they had once expelled from their town. . . . He pleaded with love, but spoke plainly the whole truth. The consequences can be easily anticipated. Filled with fanatic fury at his boldness, and unable to reply to his arguments, the populace seized him, and dragged him out of the town: there by the command, or at least the connivance, of the king, he was stoned on the 30th of June 1315. [21]

This oft-repeated story of martydom for Christ is a graphic illustration of "finding your life through losing it" (Matthew 16:25)—in contrast to losing life's meaning through self-indulgence or by "keeping your options open" and committing to nothing or anyone.

The number of Christian martyrs in this 20th

century has already exceeded the number of all the Christian martyrs in all the other centuries *combined*. Global evangelical news agencies report that each year an estimated 156,000 Christians are killed for their faith. Nearly *two thirds* of the world's population currently lives under regimes that still persecute Christians for their faith.

A Few Pleas to Pastors

A comment occasionally heard in church and mission circles is: "I was very interested in missions, but my pastor felt I was in too responsible a position in the church to leave. He said there is too much work to do right here, even though, of course, he supports missions." A pastor's job is to lead the church by word and example. The missions movement and its development in the church will go forward only if *initiated, directed,* and *modeled* by the leadership. The pastor must act, as well as preach, missions. Concerning his philosophy of ministry, Gene Garrick, formerly pastor of Tabernacle Church in Norfolk, Virginia, wrote:

> *Without pastoral concern,* missions interest will lag. It is probably the single most important element to a missionary-sending church. My commitment to missions impacts my philosophy of ministry, my understanding of the nature and purpose of the church, and the priority of missions in light of the whole purpose of God as revealed in the Scripture. The pastor must lead the missions program in a very real sense. . . . He must not simply accept it as a part of the program, but as a major item on the agenda of the church. [22]

John R. Mott, famous for his work with the Student Volunteer Movement which sent thousands of missionaries to the field, said:

> Each church needs something to live for apart from itself and its own local work. Nothing short of participation in the sublime undertaking of the evangelization of the world is adequate to emancipate from selfishness, and to call out the best energies of mind and heart. [23]

Pastors and other local church leaders are God's instruments for taking the church from being a *reservoir* of God blessings to being an unselfish *channel* for transmitting God's life and blessing to the world. Those who are being trained for ministry should seek out courses that provide a solid biblical foundation of missions such as the "Perspectives on the World Christian Movement" taught in many North American cities. Evangelism and missions should be a requirement of every seminary. Outreach in the local church community, as well as to the peoples of the world, is a significant aspect of a pastor's calling to ministry.

Most mission agencies are strongly supportive of local church pastors visiting their missionaries on the field. The counsel pastors can give often greatly benefits the missionary, who realizes the pastor knows him or her and has his or her best interests at heart. The inspiration pastors receive from both missionaries and national Christians, and the exposure to the spiritual needs of other areas of the world they experience, typically has a *life-changing effect.* ACMC suggests that anyone with a heart for missions who travels overseas should offer to take his pastor along. These and other reasons to travel abroad—including trips by short-term teams—provide invaluable insight into the "reality" of mission's need, opportunity and fruitfulness.

A second plea to pastors: Mission agencies speak a great deal of how dependent they are upon the churches. This dependency goes well beyond money and people. More fundamentally, the church is the foundational *forming* instrument in the life of her members. *Mission agencies can use only those people whom God has fashioned and prepared for His service through faithful preaching, training and modeling in a church body.* From the mission agency point of view, there will be questions about the suitability of a person for cross-cultural ministry if he or she has not already played a vital role in the ministry of the local church. "If their church wouldn't miss them, we probably wouldn't want them" is the position our co-workers on the fields take! Unless the church calls and demonstrates to her members a servant lifestyle aimed away from self-centeredness, there is little hope that mission agencies will export an incarnational gospel worthy of the kingdom of God.

Part of the tension a church faces involves the loss of key members of that church fellowship when commissioned by the congregation to act as their instruments in reaching the world. But obedience to the Great Commission also brings blessing, for as the church extends its ministry worldwide new members will surely be brought into the participation of ministry in the church at home.

Another plea to those in church leadership: A recent phenomenon is the number of books being published that deal with healing from damage wrought by "spiritually abusive" church leaders. Such material can be helpful to any who have gone through bad church experiences and are left with feelings of guilt and failure. John White, author of *The Fight* and *Eros Redeemed*, declares that spiritual abuse presents evils which are real, widespread and deadly. *My* concern, however, is that in an effort to avoid spiritually abusive authority and/or manipulation, pastors and spiritual leaders may hesitate to present clearly the biblical call to selfless service for Jesus. For, in *Healing Spiritual Abuse*, Ken Blue writes:

> There is a kind of dehumanizing spiritual abuse that is actually worse than the misuse of God's law. It is expressed in the ill-defined calls to "enter into the deeper life," to "lay it all on the altar," to "surrender," to "yield," and so on. If these calls are not defined or explained, they can never be put to rest in our conscience. The question sensitive hearts perpetually ask is, "Have I yielded or surrendered enough?" This establishes permanent guilt feelings and exchanges salvation by God's grace for salvation through my surrender, in which I can never rest. [24]

Unquestionably, the dangers Blue suggests are real. My wife and I spent a number of years under a pastor who identified himself with Moses and believed church members should obey his revelations and direction as if from Sinai. Passages like Romans 6 were used to emphasize the lack of rights a "crucified"

Christian possesses and to thereby justify imposing *his* will on others. Years of fruitful, exciting ministry among university students were undermined by his unbiblical authoritarianism. As a result, I *agree* with Blue that terms like "surrender" and "yielding to the Lord" must be defined in the context of the grace of God, and our service seen as the joyful privilege of people who have been transformed by Him.

However, it should be kept in mind that terms such as "yielding our all to the Lord" and "surrendering our desires to His" *have a biblical basis.* (See Romans 6 and 2 Chronicles 30:8.) It is unfortunate that the classic deeper-life teaching of ones such as Andrew Murray, calling for "surrender" of our self-centeredness, seems for the most part *lost* in our churches today.

Let me include an example of Andrew Murray's writings:

> We have suggested here the possibility of two types of Christian life. There may be a life partly under the law and partly under grace; or a life entirely under grace, in the full liberty from self-effort and the full experience of the divine strength which it can give. A true beliver may still be living partly under the law, in the power of self-effort, striving to do what he cannot accomplish. The continued failure in his Christian life which he admits is due to this one thing: *He trusts in himself and tries to do his best.* He does, indeed, pray and look to God for help, but still it is he in his strength, helped by God, who is to do the work.

In the Epistles to the Romans, Corinthians, and Galatians, Paul tells believers that they have not received the spirit of bondage again, that they are free from the law, that they are no more servants but sons. He warns them to beware of becoming entangled again with the yoke of bondage. . . .

They do not know that all failure can have but one cause: *Men seek to do themselves what grace alone can do in them,* what grace most certainly will do. . . .

There again you have the twofold Christian life. The one, in which that "not I"—I am nothing, I can do nothing—has not yet become a reality. The other, when the wondrous exchange has been made and grace has taken the place of our effort. Then we say and know, "I live; yet not I, but Christ liveth in me." It may then become a lifelong experience. "The grace of our Lord was exceeding abundant with faith and love which is in Christ Jesus." [25]

Unfortunately, North American ministry of late has tended to center primarily around the needs of *church members* rather than responding to and pleasing *God.* David Rambo, president of The Christian and Missionary Alliance, has challenged his ministerial colleagues, calling them to experience and emphasize the truth of "death to self" as an irreplaceable truth in their ministry. He agrees that this truth has frequently been distorted but, "the pendulum has swung, as usually happens, to the opposite extreme. Narcissism, or love of self, and the age of 'me' have come roaring into our culture. The church, often unwittingly, has poured holy water on this deviant philosophy. . . . Jesus is not a value-added commodity to dress up the self-life. He is a replacement for an ugly self-absorption that robs us of the Christ-life and makes our walk with God a mere shadow of what it could be." [26]

Rambo goes on to quote C.S. Lewis from *Mere Christianity*:

> Christ says, "Give me All. I don't want so much of your time and so much of your work: I want You. I have not come to torment your natural self, but to kill it. No half-measures are any good. I don't want to cut off a branch here and there, I want to have the whole tree down. Hand over the whole natural self, all the desires which you think innocent as well as the ones you think wicked—the whole outfit. I will give you a new self instead. In fact, I will give you Myself: my own will shall become yours." [27]

Imagine, Rambo suggests, if a church (or mission agency) was full of people who have willingly experienced the cross and are now enjoying resurrection benefits by faith! Meeting personal needs would no longer be primary, while meeting the needs of the world and developing intimacy with God would be *paramount*.

The church should be a means to an end: that of growing mature, whole disciples of Christ who will live evangelistic lives here and abroad. The pastor "ought to be pastoring a center for world evangelization. They are not simply taking care of a flock of people. . . . Missions and evangelism is the task of the church." [28]

Lastly, beware the present "fad" defining missions too broadly. Missionary statesman Stephen Neill has wisely said, "If everything is mission—nothing is mission." The word "missionary" comes from the root Latin word *missio* which means "a sending," and has always referred to sending people from one culture, on a mission, to another. A popular remark at today's typical mission-related event is "we are all missionaries." Though this remark may originate from the pure motive of desiring that each Christian recognize his or her responsibility to be a witness and proclaimer of Jesus and His gospel, *there is an important technical and practical distinction*. Why ignore the significant difference between those who stay home and present Jesus as evangelists and those "sent ones" who go cross-culturally as missionaries?

Missionary types squirm when someone says, "All Christians are missionaries." Is the title "missionary" held in such high esteem that a Christian's significance is linked to that title? Do we have to be *titled* a missionary to feel fully Christian? Of course not! Is everyone titled "pastor" because we are all called to care for and minister to each other? The distinctive term "missionary" should be reserved for those who are the "sent ones" from the church, to go cross-culturally to plant churches in the name of Jesus. At the same time, we should continue to challenge every Christian to be an effective *witness* for Jesus wherever he or she is.

CHAPTER THREE

Doctrinal Uncertainty in a Tolerant Society—How Essential Is the Gospel?

"... pluralism means—everyone affirms his values and we all live with civic equality and tolerance. That's my dream. But in public school, Jews don't meet Christians. Christians don't meet Hindus. Everybody meets nothing. That is, as I explain to Jews all the time, why their children so easily intermarry. Jews don't marry Christians. Non-Jewish Jews marry non-Christian Christians. Jews for nothing marry Christians for nothing. They get along because they affirm nothing. They have everything in common—nothing."—Jewish author Dennis Prager

"The greatest ones in any nation will contradict their generation." —G.K. Chesterton

"Ninety percent of Americans say they believe in God. Yet the urgent sense of personal sin has all but disappeared in the current upbeat style in American religion. ... In earlier eras, ministers regularly exhorted congregations to humbly 'confess our sins.' But the aging baby boomers who are rushing back to church do not want to hear sermons that might rattle their self-esteem."—Kenneth L. Woodward, *Newsweek*, February 6, 1995

3

Tolerance has become an icon in the West. At all costs, in all discussion and judgment assertions, anything short of a completely tolerant and accepting attitude is not tolerated. "It may not be my thing, but hey, who am I to judge?" This non-judgmental attitude has had its leavening effect upon not only our society but also the church's thoughts about sin and guilt.

"We've gotten to the point where to 'be compassionate' is to refrain from judgment," says David Blankenhorn of the Institute for American Values in New York. "That's antithetical to our whole moral tradition." Blankenhorn is puzzled by the unevenness of our society's judgments. "We are a society that doesn't mind making people feel bad about certain behavior: smoking, drugs, racially denigrating language," Blankenhorn notes. "But on sexuality and procreation—the heart of the social crisis—there's a reluctance to judge. . . . The challenge is to combine shame with empathy . . . to draw a line between right and wrong so bright it can be seen forever. Risk ridicule. Think anew."[1]

The *National and International Religion Report* of September 19, 1994, states that nearly all Americans (95 percent) believe in God, and four out of five describe themselves as Christians. However, of those self-described "Christians," 1 percent do not believe in God, 11 percent do not believe in life after death, 13 percent do not believe in miracles, 15 percent don't accept the virgin birth, 23 percent do not believe in hell.

The non-judgmental tolerance theme has affected not only our culture but also our theology, and not simply among those questioned in man-on-the-street surveys. Many leading evangelicals question God's eternal judgment and wrath against sin and sinners, causing Robertson McQuilkin to claim that this is probably one of the most harmful agents undermining the missionary enterprise.

Consequently, American evangelicals seem increasingly uncertain about the appropriateness of leaving their culture and moving into another culture to evangelize. Horror stories of ethnocentric Westerners engaging in "cultural disruption" abound. "Isn't our judgment of what may be right or wrong about another culture suspect?" some would argue. "Shouldn't our compassion be limited to sending funds to relieve obvious suffering? Let's not lose sleep when it comes to questionable matters like eternal judgment." As a result, there is much hesitancy among some Christians about cross-cultural ministry.

Affirming the evangelical position that Christ is man's only hope but denying eternal punishment for those not believing in Him has become increasingly popular. Devotees of "feel good" preaching, reincarnation, and other new age concepts belittle the reality of guilt. Some religionists propose that, because God is loving and just, hell—if there is such—will purify sin from man, and in the end God will bring everyone to glory. Others claim that while not everyone will be saved, sinners will not experience eternal, conscious punishment because the fires of judgment will completely annihilate those who reject Christ. Annihilationism takes literally the statement that "sin is self-destructive." (See footnote [2] , on page 199, for a list of eight current books dealing with this subject.)

Missionary motivation has traditionally arisen from the combination of Christ's clear command in Matthew 28 and a genuine concern for lost souls. Doctrinal shifts toward versions of universalism and annihilationism undermine missionary urgency. Quite apart from this, these doctrines contradict the clear teaching of Scripture passages which assert the endless punishment of the wicked:

> "As the new heavens and the new earth that I make will endure before me," declares the Lord, "so will your name and descendants endure. From one New Moon to another and from one Sabbath to another, all mankind will come and bow down before me," says the Lord. "And they will go out and look upon the dead bodies of those who rebelled against me; their worm will not die, nor will their fire be quenched, and they will be loathsome to all mankind." (Isaiah 66:22–24)

> "If your hand causes you to sin, cut it off. It is better for you to enter life maimed than with two hands to go into hell, where the fire never goes out. And if your foot causes you to sin, cut it off. It is better for you to enter life crippled than to have two feet and be thrown into hell. And if your eye causes you to sin, pluck it out. It is better for you to enter the kingdom of God with one eye than to have two eyes and be thrown into hell, where 'their

worm does not die, and the fire is not quenched.'" (Mark 9:43–48)

Empathetic concern for the human soul and emphasis on the loving nature of God make eternal punishment in hell a difficult concept to embrace. While taking courses at Regent College in Vancouver, Canada, under Dr. J.I. Packer, I was moved afresh as I considered the biblical data on eternal judgment and the implications of an eternity of punishment separated from God's goodness. In one sense, this concept is more than we can assimilate. No doubt the staggering considerations of such a doctrine have led some to abandon it. In a dialogue on this topic, Clark Pinnock made the following statement:

> I was led to question the traditional belief in everlasting conscious torment because of moral revulsion and broader theological considerations, not first of all on scriptural grounds. It just does not make any sense to say that a God of love will torture people forever for sins done in the context of a finite life. . . . It's time for evangelicals to come out and say that the biblical and morally appropriate doctrine of hell is annihilation, not everlasting torment. [3]

John Stott sets forth his reasoned defense for annihilationism in *Evangelical Essentials: A Liberal-Evangelical dialogue* (InterVarsity). In complete candor he says:

> Emotionally, I find the concept ["eternal conscious torment"] intolerable and do not understand how people can live with it without either cauterizing their feelings or cracking under the strain. But our emotions are a fluctuating, unreli-

able guide to truth and must not be exalted to the place of supreme authority in determining it. As a committed Evangelical, my question must be—and is—not what does my heart tell me, but what does God's word say? [4]

Dr. Packer, in his "Doctrine of Eschatology" course, referred to annihilationism and universalism as aberrational, and sternly reminded students that speculation about such matters outside of Scripture, on the basis of personal emotion, is dangerous. In class he reminded us that, though theories of salvation through non-Christian religions and of unbelievers being annihilated abound, evangelical Protestants have historically maintained the unending agony of those who leave this world without Jesus Christ. In *The Bible and the Future*, Anthony Hoekema writes:

> If we take the testimony of Scripture seriously, and if we base our doctrines on its teachings—as indeed we should—we are compelled to believe in the eternal punishment of the lost. To be sure, we shrink from this teaching with all that is within us, and do not dare to try to visualize how this eternal punishment might be experienced by someone we know. But the Bible teaches it and we must accept it. [5]

Certainly God does not desire that anyone should perish (2 Peter 3:9), and He has provided the means by which man may have fellowship with Him for eternity. Man is also free to make "hellish" choices here, rejecting the life and benefits of God's goodness in Christ, and Scripture says he will experience the consequences of those choices. "As C.S. Lewis has put it, sin is man's saying to God throughout life, 'Go away and leave me alone.' Hell is God's finally saying to man, 'You may have your wish.' It is God's leaving man to himself, as man has chosen." [6]

A third and very speculative approach receiving current attention is the question of whether or not people must physically and intelligently hear (or read) the good news about Jesus Christ in order to be saved. Is conscious faith in Christ and knowledge of the gospel a definite prerequisite for salvation? Some evangelicals think that in the same way that Old Testament persons could receive salvation through the benefits of Christ's yet-to-come atoning death on the cross (established, of course, from the foundation of the world), so people *today* beyond the hearing of the gospel may also receive the benefit of Christ's death *without a conscious knowledge* of the name of Jesus Christ—a salvation based instead on their response to the light they have about God. This belief obviously poses the danger of "cutting the nerve of urgency in the missionary cause."

Theological discourse regarding this difficult topic continues. Clark Pinnock, in his book *No Other Name Under Heaven*, affirms that only through the person and work of Christ will God admit guilty sinners into His presence, but interprets Acts 4:12 ("There is no other name . . . by which we must be saved") as referring to the work finished and accepted by the Father even if the sinner is *unaware* of this atonement. Through this work, God gazes upon a repentant human whether or not he or she has heard of Christ, and judges that individual according to that one's response to the light of conscience.

This is the position taken by Norman Anderson in his book *The World's Religions.* He writes:

> May this not provide us with a guideline to the solution of the burning problem of those in other religions who have never heard—or never heard with understanding—of the Saviour? . . . What if the Spirit of God convicts them, as he alone can, of something of their sin and need; and what if he enables them, in the darkness or twilight, somehow to cast themselves on the mercy of God and cry out, as it were, for his forgiveness and salvation? Will they not then be accepted and forgiven in the one and only Saviour? . . . It cannot be claimed that this is the clear and unequivocal teaching of the New Testament, where the primary emphasis is on the Christian's duty to share the Good News of God's love with the whole world. . . . But if this is true—as I myself believe—then it certainly does not lessen the Christian's missionary responsibility. . . . His Master's last commission and command was that he should go and tell the Good News, and that should be quite enough. . . . Any who are enabled by the Holy Spirit to turn to God, in the twilight, in repentance and faith, would still, moreover, lack that assurance, conscious companionship and confident message which come only from a knowledge that Christ died to justify his people, rose again to manifest himself to them in the "power of an endless life" and has commissioned them as his ambassadors to appeal to others to be reconciled to God. So it is our manifest duty to share this knowledge, and these privileges, with all mankind. [7]

Though tantalizing, this position has one major problem: it does not give adequate recognition to the importance of the *name* of the Lord. Hearing and believing on the name of the Lord is stressed in the New Testament. Romans 10:13–14 says, "Everyone who calls on the name of the Lord will be saved. How, then, can they call on the one they have not believed in? And how can they believe in the one of whom they have not heard? And how can they hear without someone preaching to them?" Such texts might provide us room for a measure of speculation, hoping that salvation extends beyond Christ's name and rudimentary gospel knowledge. But with insufficient scriptural evidence, as well as lack of historical examples of men and women living in salvation apart from explicit knowledge of Christ, it seems perilous to place much hope in Anderson's theory.

Theologian Millard Erickson (*Christian Theology*) believes with Anderson that some may be judged on the basis of their response to the light they have without actually hearing the name of Jesus. But he states emphatically that this does not undermine the missionary mandate.

> Nor is the motivation for the missionary enterprise undercut by this position. If what has been said here thus far is correct, then what Paul is saying in the remainder of Romans is that very few, if any, actually come to such a saving knowledge of God on the basis of the natural revelation alone. . . . Thus, the effect of this revelation is simply to make them responsible and hence rightfully condemnable. . . . In view of this it is urgent

that the gospel message be taken to them, thus increasing the likelihood and improving the opportunity of their entering into the relationship which is requisite for true fellowship with the Father. If they are really to have a chance for faith, we must inform them. [8]

Dr. Helen Roseveare, a WEC medical missionary who served in Africa for many years, now travels worldwide speaking on behalf of missions. She is frequently asked about the necessity of sinners hearing the name of Christ as an essential element of salvation. She answers emphatically that "in the end God is the judge and will certainly judge justly, but for now, in this life on earth, the Bible clearly teaches that the lost are lost (2 Corinthians 4:3–6) and that Christ commands Christians to *go* to them and proclaim the gospel that 'Jesus Christ died for our sins' (1 Corinthians 15:3)—and that 'We are His ambassadors' (2 Corinthians 5:19). In all the theological debate, our one concern is obedience to Christ's command." [9]

In this era of ethical and biblical tolerance and ambiguity, we must insist that scripture be interpreted by scripture, not by the world's consciousness of constantly shifting cultural themes. We must steadfastly refrain from forcing the message of Scripture to accommodate any cultural ideology, whether on the right or left, politically correct or politically incorrect. The Scriptures stand in judgment over every cultural ideology. To be sure, God *is* speaking to us in these times; but it is essential that we first hear the word of God in Scripture, enabling us to interpret and recognize the hand of God in these days.

Some in the evangelical community are asking questions such as "Is hell a proper motivation for missions?" Others are hoping that multitudes will be included from those who have responded to the light of conscience even though the report from misionaries is that there are few they have found who seemed to be in this "enlightened" condition. Rather, it is the gospel message that produces the faith enabling the experience of salvation. Romans 1:16 states that "the gospel . . . is the power of God for salvation of everyone who believes."

As Christians, we must resolve to reach those who have never heard the gospel. Despite the reproach of an increasingly secular world, we must continue to plant churches among all peoples, so that everyone may have a chance to glorify the One who created them and sent his Son to purchase their redemption.[10]

CHAPTER FOUR

Family Life and Children's Welfare: Is It Safe Over There?

"If God has fit you to be a missionary, I would not have you shrivel down to be a king."— Charles H. Spurgeon to his son

"Missionary families, no less than any other families, are dear to the heart of God. God does not require a dichotomizing or prioritizing of responsibilities along the axis of ministry versus family. Neglect of family is not part of a bargain one strikes with God." —Ted Ward, *International Bulletin of Missionary Research*

The bottom line has to do with the will of God. To raise children in the place of God's appointment is safer by far than to seek the ideal environment outside the will of God.—Source unknown

Sections of this chapter are extracted from an unpublished manuscript written in 1992 by my wife
Judy, entitled "Family *or* Ministry?"

4

Well-meaning friends and relatives warn us that taking our children away from their home country and away from grandma and friends will ruin their lives. We sometimes hear stories of a "missionary kid" who did not fare well in life or who rejected the Lord. Discussion about a family moving overseas for mission work can therefore generate the following responses:

"My family is my number one priority!"

"I know a man whose ministry destroyed his family!"

"We would NEVER send our children away to boarding school!"

"God expects parents to teach their own children!"

Care to provoke a discussion among American Christians that's guaranteed to raise blood-pressure levels and inspire full and emotional participation? *Family vs. ministry* is the topic!

Most of the "horror" stories we have heard of children who grew up to rebel against the Christian faith seem to concern those who felt neglected and pushed aside by the demands of their parents' ministry. In reaction to such cases, a new approach has become common during the early years of the '90s, one which poses a major problem for mission agencies: applicants insist that their *families* are their *number one* priority, with ministry coming in a poor second.

Ruth Tucker, author of the mission history *From Jerusalem to Irian Jaya*, comments: "Today family concerns are paramount in the minds of potential missionaries and missionaries already on the field. And the plight of missionary kids (MKs), once a peripheral issue, has become a key factor in shaping the future of world evangelism." [1]

Young parents schooled by sermons and radio broadcasts of "family theology" are having second thoughts about bringing up their children in the uncertainties of a foreign environment.

Many missions leaders are concerned by what they perceive to be an almost exclusive emphasis on the health of the family and the individual. **"Family has become god in many churches, thereby throttling many potential missionaries,"** writes *Evangelical Missions Quarterly* editor James Reapsome. "Some churches are putting the married state, home comfort, and the education and happiness of children before world evangelization." [2]

A nebulous feeling that missionaries of an earlier day thoughtlessly sacrificed their children for their work is prevalent in the minds of many in America's churches. Those who feel called to missions are often determined that there will be no possibility of this happening in their own families! A study done recently for Wycliffe Bible Translators concludes that "Family occupies a different place in the thinking of today's young adult. Whereas past generations of mission workers considered that the whole family was called to the task, and children were part of the price (at times to the sacrifice of the family and detriment of the children), today's young parents place a high priority on family life and care, not wanting their children to suffer or be deprived."[3] Dan Harrison, of IVF, adds, "In missions today, we are seeing an apparent change in attitude by new missionaries with young children, who in increasing numbers feel that their kids come first and the work second."[4]

Is it possible to set up such a system of priorities—kids first, the work second—and to make all decisions on that basis and at the same time serve the Lord unreservedly? Admittedly, to do God's work at the expense of the family can lead to disaster for the children. But to place such an emphasis on the family that no sacrifice to accomplish God's work is acceptable can lead to a life of spiritual barrenness.

What has caused this emotionally-charged issue to become a divisive force, creating misunderstanding and strong emotions? The advocates of "family theology" in the United States have developed their system of thought from a few basic premises. One of these is, of course, that family comes *first* on the priorities list. The problem with this position, however, is that if anything other than *God* comes first, we are guilty of idolatry. Family theology easily turns into *family idolatry* because of this belief that family is the most important priority in life.

But will evangelical "environmental determinism" protect our children and produce what God wants in their lives?

As Dr. Raymond Chester of UFM puts it, "We seem to want to worship anything but God—even something as worthwhile as the family."[5] Dr. Chester agrees that we have all seen examples of men and women who have damaged their families by putting ministry first, but he proposes that in reaction to this problem many Christians have fallen into another unbalanced position by declaring that family is the key thing to consider in our service for the Lord. Is it not a fact that with sincere hearts most of us as young parents have taken our children forward in a church service and dedicated them to the Lord? "Yet a strange and very serious phenomenon then takes place, as I observe it," says Dr. Chester. "We seem to snatch these children back off the altar. We look up at God and say, 'Keep your hands off him; he's mine. Don't you dare touch my child!'"[6]

The family was established by God to bring new people into the world, to provide for them, to prepare them for adult life, to teach them His ways. A loving Christian family is a precious gift from God. Yet this is the same God who gave the Great Commission, and how often we see His gift become His rival in our devotion! How many times do we hear, "I'm willing to go overseas, of course, but how could I expose my children to all the disease?" or "We believe God is calling us to be pioneer church planters, but we could only do that if there are just the right local educational opportunities for our children."

What are we teaching our kids? Are we letting them apprehend, from their personal lives as well as through formal teaching, that God truly is sovereign? That God is *God*? If we proclaim a God who is sovereign but live as though *we* are sovereign in their lives, we are creating a difficulty. We act as though *we* are their total protection. *We* will keep them from disease. *We* will keep them from harm. *We* will keep them from the influences of this dirty society or that disease-filled nation over there. Then we wonder why they faithlessly buckle under pressure! Can we not see how our lifestyle is opposed to what we preach? What we are really saying is, "I can't allow anyone to interfere with my family because *I* am God over my family." Certainly we have been given the commission to raise our children in the teachings of Scripture and protect them, but not as the primary resource and the ultimate line of defense. That is the responsibility of *God*.

The commands of our Lord include His commission to "Therefore go and make disciples of all nations, baptizing them in the name of the Father and of the Son and of the Holy Spirit"(Matthew 28:19) and "If anyone comes to me and does not hate his father and mother, his wife and children, his brothers and sisters—yes, even his own life—he cannot be my disciple"(Luke 14:26) and "Everyone who has left houses or brothers or sisters or father or mother or children or fields for my sake will receive a hundred times as much and will inherit eternal life" (Matthew 19:29).

What should we be saying to these parents, who are considering the world of missions, in whose minds "negative images loom large, especially in regard to their 'helpless' children who are assumed to be harmed in some way by the parents' decision to follow Christ? All they can imagine for their children is the dark side of the moon." [7]

First, it must be clearly emphasized that "missionary families, no less than any other families, are dear to the heart of God. God does not require a dichotomizing or prioritizing of responsibilities along the axis of ministry versus family. One's family is *part* of one's ministry. *Neglect of family is not part of a bargain one strikes with God.*" [8]

Second, it must be recognized that life's priorities do not line up in neat 1,2,3 fashion. But they do all fall naturally into their rightful places as we put God *first* in everything. Careful seeking of His will and a faith-filled response to what He shows will enable us to walk His path for us. His will for us in His service necessarily takes into account the families He gives us, and we can trust Him to love them and care for every need. We need to share this with prospective missionaries and challenge them to all-out faith. "In the current discussions of the conditions and choices that confront missionaries, one has the uneasy feeling that God is assumed to be either whimsical or senile: calling husbands but not wives; and worse, forgetting altogether that those He has called may also have some responsibilities to their children. Perhaps faulty theology lies behind some part of the contemporary anxiety about the missionary's family." [9]

We also need to help prospective missionaries realize that the current "family" phenomena is in many ways an overreaction to both problems of the past and the deterioration of morals and family life in our society. It seems that, in reaction to the practice of ministry taking preeminence over the family, there has been a tendency to go to the other extreme and treat the family as an end in itself.

We need to make a greater effort to educate the Church about the needs of the unreached and the implications thereof for missionary families. We need also to clearly counteract the impact of extreme teachings— such as the fable that any separation from children for even brief periods is injurious, and the fiction that taking our children out of this country is dangerous. Actually, many North American missionary parents have discovered that their home country, with its creeping immorality, is far more dangerous and a bigger challenge to proper child-rearing than the more "primitive" areas where God has sent them.

Is obedience to God's command to go into all the world and preach the gospel incompatible with having a secure, biblical family life?

In the book *A Boy's War*, we read the true story of David Michell who, as a young MK, was separated from his parents and held in a Japanese concentration camp during World War II. The book includes glimpses of the *Chariots of Fire* hero Eric Liddell but is primarily the story of a young boy's agonizing separation from his parents—and of God's faithfulness. In his foreword to the book, Daniel Bacon, the U.S. Director of the Overseas Missionary Fellowship (OMF), asks the following:

Are they really compatible—God's design for the family and His call to world evangelism?

Far from being merely a question for classroom debate, this is a question for which potential missionaries and supporting churches increasingly demand answers.

Given the breakdown of family life in Western countries, with rampant divorce, single parents, working mothers, absentee fathers, etc., Christians are right to place fresh emphasis on God's plan for the home. Not surprisingly, parents preparing for missionary service struggle with guilt about the legitimacy of taking children overseas. Many wrestle with the hard issues of how they can both serve in their missionary calling and at the same time meet the needs of their family.

Missionary societies know that this is an important area. Enabling families to cope overseas, with the inevitable demands and risks that missionary life entails, absorbs considerable time, energy, and expense. The whole matter has, in fact, become a major inter-mission concern and has spawned a number of helpful programs and resources in recent years to assist families to face cross-cultural living and ministry.

Yet there are times in the life of a missionary family when things don't go as planned and when circumstances seem out of control even in the wake of the seminars and preparation. Should the risks to our family keep us from moving ahead? Where should we draw the line between responsible action for the welfare of the family and obedience to the claims of the Great Commission?

Our Lord warned that true discipleship would not be without cost, nor obedience to the Great Commission without its price. We need to keep this perspective. Whatever the cost, however, I am convinced both as a parent and as a counselor/friend to other missionary families that God's design and care for the family and His call to world evangelism are not incompatible. Through the trauma of war, separation from parents, and deprivation we see God's faithfulness and His ability to meet the deepest needs of His children. [10]

One of the most moving missionary stories I have ever heard was told during a missions conference by David Michell about his return from the prisoner-of-war camp in China and seeing his parents in Australia for the first time in six years. The dockside reunion provided a moving picture of hugs, tears and gratefulness for the faithfulness of God. It is amazing to see how the author not only survived his ordeal, but that in time he served as a missionary in Japan, with all the implications for his own young family, and today is an active *proponent* of families in missions.

Following in their parents' footsteps is not uncommon among MKs. Steve Richardson, son of Don Richardson of *Peace Child* fame, grew up in Irian Jaya. When he was a baby, his father left in a dugout canoe to make contact with the Sawi tribe. Steve, a graduate of Columbia Bible College, is following a similar calling and is himself initiating a work to another unreached tribe.

Many young parents draw back from missionary commitment from fear their children will suffer. Historically and statistically, the opposite is the case. The children of missionaries have been successful spiritually, emotionally, socially, and vocationally in far higher proportions than the children of parents in other vocations.

In any event, *the bottom line has to do with the will of God.* To raise children in the place of God's appointment is *safer by far* than to seek the ideal environment outside the will of God.

Most mission agencies make every effort to provide a wide range of educational options for children, including international schools, local national schools, boarding and nonboarding schools, homeschooling,* correspondence courses, and tutors. Of these options, the missionary boarding school seems to receive the most indignant response from North American parents. Our experience as personnel directors fielding questions on this subject leaves us with the impression that most American parents see wild images when boarding school is mentioned. In contrast to this caricature, those young people and parents from a missionary-boarding-school background with whom we have contact have spoken *very highly* of the experience.

---

*There is a growing North American movement crusading on behalf of Christian homeschooling. Homeschooling can be a legitimate educational alternative for some families based on abilities of the parent/teacher, homeschool materials utililized, availability of other schooling alternatives, the makeup of the child socially and academically, etc. A problem can develop, though, and has on some mission fields, when North Americans arrive with a "homeschooling hobby horse"and attempt to convince other Christian parents that homeschooling is the *only* genuinely Christian form of education for a child. At that point this otherwise legitimate educational alternative enters the legalistic category. Those who don't join the crusade are considered less than fully responsible Christian parents. On an international team there will be some families whose home country does not accept homeschooling as a viable academic option and some parents who do not feel capable of homeschooling their children. If pressure/ guilt about parental responsibility in regard to homeschooling is exerted, it tends to be divisive for the missionary team.

As a result, we attempt to present an objective, factual look at boarding school to defuse the emotive response—sometimes successfully and sometimes not. Ruth Tucker states, "The idea that boarding school has a negative effect on missionary children has not held up." [11]

One study (the results are given on following pages) found self-esteem higher among boarding-school MKs who had spent some years separated from their parents than among those who had spent fewer years away from their parents. Another common theme found in studies of MKs is that they tend to be high achievers and intellectually more advanced than their non-MK peers.

Surveys done over the years indicate that the vast majority of MKs, in spite of their frustrations, would not have chosen a different lifestyle. Of course, modern transportation has now made it possible for MKs who attend boarding school to spend time with their parents between each school term, and sometimes even more often.

What effects does going to boarding school have on MKs?

"Boarding school was the best experience and growing-up potential that was available. I'm sorry for all who didn't have the opportunities I did." . . . "I look upon my MK experience as a blessing and a great privilege. I wouldn't trade it for anything."

Recently an unpublished survey was done by UFM researcher Larry Sharp among 533 adult children of missionaries to Brazil (268 boarders, 262 nonboarders) from a variety of missions, denominations, and schools in Brazil. The mean number of years in boarding school was five. Here are the results:

1. As adults, MKs who boarded are more likely to be religiously committed. They read the Bible, share their faith, and give a tithe more often than non-boarders.

2. Boarding-experienced MKs are more likely to feel at home in Brazil and want their children to be raised in Brazil.

3. As adults, boarders are more likely to have missions as a career goal and are three times more likely to return overseas as missionaries.

4. Boarders are more likely to have had a teacher who had a powerful influence on their direction in life.

5. Boarders are more satisfied with "meaning and purpose in life."

6. Boarders are more politically conservative than nonboarders.

In the Brazil study 98.1 percent of the adults with MK boarding school experience, from a wide range of mission backgrounds, educational experiences and present walks of life, indicate, "If I could do it all over again, I would choose to grow up as I did."

Some statistical results of this study:

	Nonboarders	Boarders
1. Had a "very happy" childhood	62%	61%
2. Felt time parents spent with them was adequate	80%	75%
3. Read the Bible "very often"	38%	55%
4. Shared their faith "often"	31%	45%
5. Presently are missionaries	8%	24%
6. Life seems filled with despair	5%	3%
7. Felt disadvantaged compared with North American peers	6%	3%
8. Consistently and often talked with parents regarding Christian values	50%	61%

David Schipper at Rosemead Graduate School of Psychology hypothesized that a boarding school student would suffer from a lower self-concept and that the longer he boarded, the lower his self-concept would get. His study of over 500 children in Asia not only failed to support the hypothesis, but indicated the *opposite*.[12]

The *data* suggest that boarding school itself is not the problem North American Christians suspect. Statistical surveys show no significant difference (in development and attitudes) between boarders and nonboarders. Obviously, individual children react differently to boarding. Some said they initially felt isolated and alone, while others enjoyed it, and one MK wrote that she was bothered that her parents would *not* let her board, because all her friends were boarding.[13]

A source of conflict or an alternative?

There is no reason for viewing boarding school and homeschooling as systems in conflict. They are simply alternatives, both of which provide for the development of young people spiritually and academically.

Missionary children who have been boarders tend to be more intimately related to and dependent upon the family than North American teenagers. Parents clearly play a more potent role in the socialization of MKs. In the Brazil study 53.2% of the MKs responded that home life was "the most meaningful experience" for them. In contrast, a survey of more than 3,000 Canadian teenagers indicated that *peers* are a much more significant influence than parents. Boarding school teenagers are even closer in values to their parents than are MKs in general.

It would appear statistically that the boarding school experience, for most, can and does yield a positive, well-adjusted young person. If parents are called to overseas living and decide that the boarding school is right, they can rest assured that they are in good company. Yet parents need to guard against applying the same decision to all their children. The boarding school may be one good option, but it is not for everyone.

A most important ingredient in the mix of factors leading to successful boarding experience lies with the parents. If they are able to involve the children in the family's ministries, thus expressing "you are part of the team," there is likely to be a far greater acceptance of their uncommon educational and social experiences.

It is encouraging to note studies which show that adult missionary kids who grew up overseas have generally done well academically. The MK Consultant and Research Team/Committee on Research and Endowment (MK-CART/CORE) is a group of professionals and representatives from many participating missions who have gathered and analyzed extensive data on adult missionary kids (AMKs). Of the 608 who were interviewed, 94 percent attended college, 73 percent graduated, and 68 percent had finished their college studies with a grade point average of 3.0 or higher.

One thing is clear: missionary children gain a host of *advantages* connected with missionary living. The problem of a quality education, even in the boarding school, should not hinder parents considering missionary service.

From a *personal* vantage point, my own children have never attended an MK boarding school, though my eldest daughter would have liked to, based on the good reports she received from boarding friends. Our family has lived in four different countries and our children have attended 17 schools. Our oldest son, born in Britain, is presently attending college and has done very well academically. Our daughter Melanie is a high school senior and has also excelled. Our three oldest children literally have friends around the world who write and phone often. Though our kids do have difficulty answering the question "Where are you from?", teachers and friends are always fascinated to hear their stories of living in Tasmania and Vancouver, British

Columbia. Our MKs are *happy, well-adjusted, profess a Christian testimony, have a love for and fascination with people and cultures outside the U.S., and make friends easily.* As far as we able to tell, being an MK has been a *plus* for them in every way.

CHAPTER FIVE

Raising Financial Support and the Problem of Missionary Affluence

"The whole church must become a mobile misionary force, ready for a wilderness life. It is a time for us to be thinking of campaign tents rather than of cathedrals."—John Mackay

"The greatest challenge we face in ministry in Irian is the day-to-day struggle against our far superior standard of living, the status and wealth we have, in comparison to the primitive people God has given us to minister to. They clearly are aware of the "gulf between"and desire to attain to that standard of power and wealth they see in us. We sought to cut back and live more simply than most missionaries in Irian Jaya. But the struggle remains. So opposite of the example of Incarnation given us by Christ. But also easy to justify. Missionaries do it every day." — Unnamed missionary couple, quoted in Jon Bonk's *Missions and Money—Affluence as a Western Missionary Problem*

"We will reap what we sow (Gal. 6:7). Though it may take years to harvest this painful crop, some materialistic parents experience it when their own children grow up and become even more materialistic than they are. What is worse, our children may become materialistic in the ultimate sense and, like the rich young ruler, reject Jesus Christ. We must avoid materialistic bondage at all costs. We must, with an act of the will, put God first in all that we do. We must seek first His kingdom and His righteousness (Matthew 6:33)."—Gene Getz, *Real Prosperity*

5

One of the most feared elements related to a missions career, causing many would-be missionaries to falter, is the raising of financial support. The apprehensions and uncertainties associated with this venture have stopped many from taking their next step toward missions.

An underlying question is being raised by many inside and outside of missions: Do we really need all the money most agencies require as missionary support? We will attempt to deal with this question of missionary affluence first, followed by consideration of the resources available to those starting out on the deputation trail.

Do North American missionaries need the high levels of support many agencies require?

Jon Bonk attempts to deal with this question in his book, *Missions and Money—Affluence as a Western Missionary Problem*. Reaction against Western missionary affluence began early in the 20th century and continues to build in intensity. Phil Parshall, writing on the tensions Western affluence can create, quotes a Korean missionary serving in Pakistan: "I think it is significant that today's image of the Christian missionary endeavor from the Asian receptor's point of view is an image of comfort and privilege. Hence, Asians tended to reject the missionary and misunderstand his message." [1]

Experienced missionaries from the West also recognize this danger. Roger Greenway shares this experience from his personal missionary experience in an article entitled, "Eighteen Barrels and Two Big Crates: How our stuff gets in the way."

> The most embarrassing moment in my missionary career occurred near the beginning, 33 years ago when our baggage arrived in Colombo, Sri Lanka. . . . On the one hand we were excited— it was "Christmas in August" with bullocks instead of reindeer bringing wonderful things from the north. But on the other hand, there was something terribly disturbing about it. We kept saying to ourselves, "We don't need all this stuff. Why did we buy it in the first place?". . . Our neighbors turned out in force to see what the Americans were getting. As we opened the crates and barrels by the side of the house, our neighbors stared in wonderment. . . . For four months, my wife and I had been building relationships and seeking to identify with the community. . . . But then suddenly, we were discovered to be what some probably suspected we were all along—filthy rich Americans who could fill their home with every conceivable comfort and adornment. A thousand sermons could not undo the damage done that day. It would have been better for our ministry if the ship had dropped our barrels and crates in the Indian Ocean.[2]

I serve as the Missions Committee chairman for our local church. Regularly, aspiring missionaries visit our committee meetings to present their support needs. Alarmingly, those needs often exceed the average church member's salary. This creates no small tension for members of the committee. Many missionary support packages appear to include every possible financial safety net, from extensive medical coverage to funds for future education or retirement. Such financial safety nets may represent wise economic choices in North American society, but many of them are out-of-range for the average churchgoer, who is bewildered—thinking missions means sacrifice. The high support levels demanded can create an attitude of cynicism towards missionary support needs among members of the church community.

Are missionaries trying to establish a comfortable "American" existence overseas, essentially factoring out the possibility of sacrificial living? Many of today's prospective missionaries approach a career in missions with what the *Profile of a Baby Boomer* study calls "a tremendous sense of entitlement." They have a need to be cared for in the form of insurance coverages, housing opportunities, retirement, assurance that the organization constantly has their best interest at heart and is watching out for them. This survey also reports that:

> With 3,800 foreign mission sending agencies, Christian young people considering mission service have a number of options and can pick and choose the organization that offers them the "best deal.". . . The attitude of entitlement extends to God's care as well. "I am giving up everything for You; things ought to go well with me, in terms of health, finances, success." The underlying idea seems to be that the life of obedience to God is a life free from pain or deprivation. [3]

Missionary recruitment of the 1990s requires that all matters be discussed; all working conditions must be probed from the beginning. One hears these questions when discussing retirement plans, guarantees about level of support and—possibly most loudly—all sorts of demands (as mentioned in the previous chapter) on behalf of the welfare of the candidates' children. Very little is left to chance, risk or faith.

In his book *Missions and Money—Affluence as a Western Missionary Problem,* Jonathan Bonk writes, "Failure to counter wealth's insidious effects upon its missionary endeavors will ensure the continued ebb of the Western churches as a kingdom force." [4] Do the Western missionaries' high support levels, which sustain certain standards of living, insulate them from the harsh realities experienced by people to whom they seek to minister? Bonk quotes Philip Slater on the North American lifestyle:

> We seek a private house, a private means of transportation, a private garden, a private laundry, self-service stores, and do-it-yourself skills of every kind. . . . Even within the family, Americans are unique in their feeling that each member should have a separate room, and even a separate telephone, television, and car when economically possible. . . . What accidental contacts we do have, furthermore, seem more intrusive, not only because they are unsought but because they are unconnected with any familiar pattern of interdependence." [5]

Ways in which this attitude creeps into a missionary's frame of reference can be illustrated from my own experience. While working in Taipei, Taiwan, I met a missionary from a very affluent North American mission. In his spacious house, I observed a full-size pool table. When I jokingly questioned him about this, he said proudly, "One thing I told them I had to have if they were going to send me here was my pool table." Though this *may* be an exception, the perception of the local people is that Christianity includes extravagant luxuries. The affluent Western missionary's way of life clouds the understanding of biblical exhortations such as Hebrews 13:5: "Keep your lives free from the love of money and be content with what you have, because God has said, 'Never will I leave you; never will I forsake you.'"

Missionaries generally are highly motivated people who, compared with their church-going counterparts back home, are sacrificing a great deal. They live under stressful conditions and, through hard work, must master local dialects. Why are affluence and money allowed to distort ministry efforts?

Arguments *for* missionary affluence originated with the Victorian approach that the missionary was responsible to "appear as a civilized gentleman." Eugene A. Nida refers to a cloud of suspicion sometimes associated with any missionary attempting to identify too closely with the local poor. In the experience of a WEC missionary working in Africa, some people do not understand and even "wonder if perhaps you are mocking them," if you try to "go native." And a missionary from another agency says locals have a concept of what the Western person is like, and to gain their respect, expectations must be met by building a better house, owning a better vehicle, etc. Too close an identification with native culture can diminish standing in the community and, therefore, the credibility of the message being preached.

Strategy utilizing technology demands enormous sums of money. Sturdy vehicles, radio and television equipment, international conferences, literature, medical advances, etc., all contribute to the proclamation of the gospel. They also require tremendous revenue. Do these technological advances ultimately aid or hinder the ministry of Jesus? The rationale exists that with millions of people within reach of television and radio broadcasts, large sums of money are required to be effective in reaching them in our technological world.

For those who defend missionary affluence, the arguments are "strong, sensible and effective. Effective enough to persuade most missionaries that personal affluence, when appropriated and enjoyed with Christian moderation, is—on economic, domestic, social and strategic grounds—infinitely preferable to the alternative." [6]

Scriptures Regarding Finances

What does the New Testament have to say concerning the biblical use of personal resources? Jon Bonk characterizes its teachings as "meddlesome, unpopular, or distressing" for those whose goal is accumulating comfort, security, and wealth.

What, then, is the "flavor" of New Testament teaching about possessions and money?

Jesus' teaching:

1. Where your treasure is, there your heart will be also. (Luke 12:34)

2. Give to the one who asks you, and do not turn away from the one who wants to borrow from you. (Matthew 5:42)

3. If anyone would come after me, he must deny himself and take up his cross and follow me. For whoever wants to save his life will lose it, but whoever loses his life for me and for the gospel will save it. What good is it for a man to gain the whole world, yet forfeit his soul? (Mark 8:34–36)

4. And if you lend to those from whom you expect repayment, what credit is that to you? Even 'sinners' lend to 'sinners,' expecting to be repaid in full. But love your enemies, do good to them, and lend to them without expecting to get anything back. Then your reward will be great, and you will be sons of the Most High, because he is kind to the ungrateful and wicked. (Luke 6:34–35)

5. Following His teaching on counting the cost, leaving all to follow Him, Jesus says in Luke 14:33, "In the same way, any of you who does not give up everything he has cannot be my disciple."

6. Someone in the crowd said to Him, "Teacher tell my brother to divide the inheritance with me." Jesus replied, "Man, who appointed me a judge or arbiter between you?" Then he said to them, "Watch out! Be on your guard against all kinds of greed; a man's life does not consist in the abundance of his possessions." (Luke 12:13–15)

7. Do not be afraid, little flock, for your Father has been pleased to give you the kingdom. Sell your possessions and give to the poor. Provide purses for yourselves that will not wear out, a treasure in heaven that will not be exhausted, where no thief comes near and no moth destroys. (Luke 12:32–34)

8. No servant can serve two masters. Either he will hate the one and love the other, or he will be devoted to the one and despise the other. You cannot serve both God and Money. (Luke 16:13)

From the Epistles:

1. But godliness with contentment is great gain. For we brought nothing into the world, and we can take nothing out of it. But if we have food and clothing, we will be content with that. People who want to get rich fall into temptation and a trap and into many foolish and harmful desires that plunge men into ruin and destruction. For the love of money is a root of all kinds of evil. Some people, eager for money, have wandered from the faith and pierced themselves with many griefs. (1 Timothy 6:6–10)

2. Keep your lives free from the love of money and be content with what you have, because God has said, "Never will I leave you; never will I forsake you." (Hebrews 13:5)

3. I know what it is to be in need, and I know what it is to have plenty. I have learned the secret of being content in any and every situation, whether well fed or hungry, whether living in plenty or in want. (Philippians 4:12)

During a 1994 phone interview with Jon Bonk about the effect of his book, I asked the following question:

Q. *What effect has this book had in mission circles? Has there been much defensiveness because of people or agencies feeling threatened?*

A. Yes, I am sure there has been some defensiveness on the part of the mission community. But for the most part it seems to have been a catalyst for discussion concerning an area that most mission agencies agreed needs some change. Some, like Phil Parshall, have wanted to use the book as a tool for change at the executive level of mission agencies. He proposed a discussion of the material at a meeting of a large North American mission. Though this kind of thing may take place, I believe that really effective change in the matter of missionary affluence will take place beginning at the grassroots—missionary level— not by an executive order or pressure from outside. One large agency, for example, has allowed a group of their missionaries to develop a sort of fraternity or "order" within the mission which has as its *modus operandi* some of the lifestyle alternatives suggested in my book.

Suggestions and solutions to the problem of missionary affluence

Roland Allen was an Anglican missionary in China from 1895 to 1903. For forty years following his missions experience, he wrote on missionary principles. Much of what he wrote was not well accepted at the time, but in the intervening years the number of those who find themselves compelled to listen has increased. In the book *Missionary Methods—St. Paul's or Ours?*, he addresses finances this way:

> There seem to have been three rules which guided Paul's practice:
>
> 1. That he did *not seek* financial help for himself. . . . Though he received gifts from his converts, he was careful not to be a burden or give any appearance of moneymaking.
>
> 2. He took no financial help to those to whom he preached. . . . Every province, every church, was financially independent. He did encourage the collection for the poor saints at Jerusalem. . . . Its importance lay in its demonstration of the unity of the church. . . . [Today,] by *not avoiding* establishing a financial operation, we load our missionaries with secular business, superintendence of works, to which is often added anxiety about the supply of funds for providing and maintaining the establishment. In this way their attention is distracted from their proper spiritual work, their energy and power is dissipated, and their first contact with people whom they desire to evangelize is connected with contracts and other purely secular concerns. . . . Moreover, if a native is put in charge of a station, he naturally expects to be paid at the same rate as his white predecessor. If he is not so paid, he feels aggrieved.
>
> 3. Every church should administer *its own* funds. . . . This modern practice [of the missionary executive handling funds] is based partly upon our distrust of native honesty and partly upon our fear of congregationalism. By congregationalism I mean, of course, not the denomination so-called, but the claim of individual congregations to act as

if they were alone in the world, independently of all other Christians. But when the natives administer their own funds they will be responsible for the administration to those who supplied them. . . . By making it *our* business, we deprive our converts of a powerful educational process, break down one of the best agencies for creating a sense of mutual responsibility, and load ourselves with a vast burden which we are ill able and often ill fitted to bear.[7]

A.W. Tozer spoke prophetically to the Church about wealth and possessions:

> Our possessions should be seen for what they are, God's loan to us, and should never be considered in any sense our own. . . . The Christian who is alive enough to know himself even slightly will recognize the symptoms of this possession malady, and will grieve to find them in his own heart. If the longing after God is strong enough within him, he will want to do something about the matter. Now, what should he do? First of all he should put away all defense and make no attempt to excuse himself either in his own eyes or before the Lord. Whoever defends himself will have himself for his defense, but he will have no other. . . . Let him insist that God accept his all, that he take things out of his heart and himself reign there in power."[8]

Years ago my wife and I attended WEC pre-field orientation with a couple headed for Chad, East Africa. (*Target Earth* rates Chad among the three poorest countries in the world in most quality-of-life indexes, such as poverty, illiteracy, infant mortality, life expectancy, etc.) Later this couple, with three young children, invited us to their home for a visit before they left for Chad. We took note of the clean but simple and noticeably spartan home in which they lived, and remarked about this. They commented, light-heartedly, that this was the way God had guided them to live in preparation for their transition to life in Chad. This might not seem remarkable except that the husband is a medical doctor with significant potential annual income in the States, and the wife is the daughter of a socially prominent family in North Carolina, where both her grandfather and father have been Governor. This family made practical economic lifestyle choices to prepare for the life they are presently living—ministering and doing medical work under primitive conditions in Chad.

Contrast that with a comment made by George Murray, general director of The Evangelical Alliance Mission:

> I was at a missions conference, and a young couple said to me, "God has spoken to us. We both have our Bible training. We believe that God wants us on the mission field. There's just one little thing that stands in our way. We just bought a house and want to pay it off before we go." I said, "Well, how long will that take?" and they said, "Twenty years." That sounds funny, but it's not funny, because they did just that!
>
> They took twenty years to pay it off. They're not on the mission field today. And there's no indication that they're *heading* for the mission

field, but everybody in their evangelical church is telling them how wise they were to build equity and to buy that house.[9]

In light of the present crisis in missions, Bonk and others sympathetic to the concern about missionary affluence list several options available to us Western Christians:

1. We can choose to *give in* to the affluent pressures at work in the world, thereby losing our effectiveness and disqualifying ourselves from leadership (1 Timothy 3:2–3).

2. We can *bind* ourselves and others with so many rules and legalities regarding finances that we cause disunity in the body of Christ and restrict the healthy diversity which should be present in His body.

3. Individually and corporately, we can *choose to listen* to "what the Spirit is speaking to the church" and obey His call to not just talk about faith but "live by faith," and then obey the scriptural admonitions regarding money, possessions, and affluence as God *guides* us.

4. We can prudently *heed the admonitions* of the Lausanne Congress as it addressed the matter of a simple lifestyle. In this regard, Ralph and Roberta Winter, founders of the U.S. Center for World Missions, have encouraged the evangelical community to live by a "war time" lifestyle, enabling funds and resources to made available to the World Christian movement. Mrs. Winter, in a 1994 *Mission Frontiers* bulletin, suggests six principles:

(a) Our lifestyle must please the Lord, yet it should not, in small matters, be so shockingly different from those among whom we walk as to make unintelligible the message we wish to convey.

(b) A simple lifestyle in the U.S. can still seem extravagant to most of the people in the world. Yet our geographic isolation does not reduce our obligation in God's eyes to people at a distance.

(c) We don't really need most of the things our culture would push off on us. Once we learn to resist social pressure, it is far easier to determine what we really want or need.

(d) There ought not be any connection between what is earned and what needs to be spent. You don't buy things just because you have the money.

(e) It is much easier to adopt a simple lifestyle if you join a support group which covenants together to live on less.

(f) The foundation of the simple lifestyle is "the explosive power of a new affection." It is this [love of Christ] which dims worldly goals and makes money itself seem unimportant.[10]

In like manner, the Wesleys long ago encouraged people to "gain all you can, save all you can, and give all you can."

Living by Faith

John White discusses the subject of "living by faith" with respect to finances in his book *The Golden Cow*. He is concerned that though the term "faith missions" is often used, yet it appears that in practice faith missions tend to lean heavily upon advertising and fund-raising techniques not dissimilar from the world's. He fears that missionary support-raising methodology has become such a preoccupation and so hard-sell that some agencies might feel rather insecure if their promotional instruments were taken away.

In an earlier century, George Müller influenced Hudson Taylor (pioneer of the China Inland Mission, now OMF) to "move men's hearts through prayer to God alone" without any direct appeal to people or churches. Taylor then influenced, among others, C.T. Studd, the founder of WEC International, to enter the adventure of trusting God for finances to do His work. Though by no means the *only* biblical method for raising funds, this way certainly appeals to those tired of high-pressure Christian fund-raising.

Amy Carmichael has pointed out that there are three scriptural methods for raising support for God's work: asking God's people for money, tentmaking, and trusting God to supply by means known in advance only by Him. These are not mutually exclusive, and in fact Paul used all three.

We must, at times, examine ourselves and our organizations with brutal honesty to determine whether our methods of fund-raising have been commercialized to the point of 1) losing immediate trust in God, who has promised to provide for His children's needs in life and service, or 2) blurring the priority of ministry over finances.

A splendid example of maintaining the first priority of God's glory in ministry comes from William Martin's 1991 biography of Billy Graham. Following the extremely well-organized success of the Los Angeles Crusade, the Graham team went to Boston with less expectation because of significantly less pre-organization. But the same "revival" response seemed to occur. Martin says of Billy Graham:

> This both exhilarated and terrified him. As soon as the service ended, he called Emery and Ockenga into a room and asked them to pray "that the Lord will keep reminding me of the fact that this is all of grace and to Him is all the glory, because I realize if I take the smallest credit for anything that has happened so far, that my lips will turn to clay." Emery was astonished: "Instead of praying for the various problems we might foresee, such as *finances*, follow-up, converts, or anything else, here, after this unexpected triumph, Billy's concern was that the Lord keep His hand on him. He also wanted us to help him continue moment to moment to give God the glory. This is something we had never seen before." [11]

We must ask with John White what has led to the perception that, in contrast to the God-glorifying approach to ministry and finances which Billy Graham has taken, Christian organizations use the same manipulative *commercial* fund-raising tactics as secular corporations.

White writes:

> My next-door neighbor who recently became a Christian was bewildered at a missionary letter he received with a space at the bottom for him to indicate how much he might feel led to pledge. "I didn't think real Christianity would be like this," he explained. "It's not that I don't want to give. But this is no different from the begging letter from the community club." Was he wrong

in expecting Christianity to be different from the community club?. . . Advertising is not wrong. Persuasion is not wrong. But both become wrong either when the motive for using them is greed or when in using them we fail to treat human beings as human, ignore their dignity and view them as objects to manipulate. . . . We must face the fact that the methods we use often undermine faith in God. [12]

Before considering specific methods and resources for support raising, there are two questions we need to ask. Is God's kingdom being held back through lack of money? Might "new" approaches to finance, including the adoption of *sacrificial living*, be necessary? It would seem to be appropriate for mission agencies to begin discussing the material presented by Jon Bonk.

Suggestions for Support-Raising

1. Be certain you are comfortable with the support levels and policies of your mission of choice so that you can carry out fund-raising without any defensiveness. A sense of superiority and harsh, unfair judgmentalism about other agencies' policies must also be avoided.

2. Churches and people should be seen primarily as co-workers in the World Christian task. Granted, some individuals and churches have little interest in missions, but you can be an agent for change. Missions-active churches and individuals started somewhere! Plugging into the missions committee of your church

(or starting one) and being *a resource for missions* are ways to begin. Your *knowledge*, tactfully and sensitively expressed, can offset the average missions committee's lack of experience in missions. Try "serving before asking" whenever possible. Let the pastor know you are available for teaching Sunday School or other tasks that might assist the ministry of the church. Also look for opportunities to share with the congregation the biblical principles of missions. One way is to encourage attendance at a "Perspectives on the World Christian Movement" course coordinated through the U.S. Center for World Missions* and at ACMC (Advancing Churches in Missions Commitment) events scheduled throughout the year in various parts of the country. Rather than treating the church as a *bankroll* for your missionary plans, draw people into your heart's vision and *listen to their counsel* as you plan your steps forward.

3. Encourage pastors, missions committee personnel, and others in the congregation to visit a mission field or participate in a *short-term mission*. Take the lead in helping to organize such a trip. Mentor mission-interested young people in the church. Once a church leader has caught a global vision firsthand, he

---

* I have taken the full "Perspectives" course for graduate credit, helped teach a summarized version of the material in a church setting and attended a "Perspectives Coordinators Workshop." This exposure to such a well-presented block of mission material impressed me. I was further confirmed in my appreciation for the course following a discussion with a young couple considering a missions career. As they traced the influential factors in their missions interest, they shared that they had taken the "Perspectives" course as young Christians, and the course had been foundational in their entire outlook on life. Would that all new Christians were so influenced in their early spiritual pilgrimage.

or she can be a tremendous missions mobilizer for the rest of the church.

4. Create a *library* for the church beginning with books such as *J. Hudson Taylor, A Man in Christ; George Mueller: Delighted in God; Perspectives on the World Christian Movement; A Chance to Die—The Life and Legacy of Amy Carmichael; The Hidden Price of Greatness*; and *C.T. Studd, Cricketer and Pioneer*. In addition to consulting the bibliography at the end of this manuscript, use Paul Borthwick's *A Mind for Missions*, which contains an excellent bibliography of missions materials. ACMC also has a great deal of resource material available.

5. Seek exposure for your ministry through meetings whenever the opportunity arises. *Seize speaking opportunities*: communicating the vision and burden of your ministry is a positive activity. Undoubtedly, the possibility of support will enter your mind in relation to ministry efforts—that's a natural thought; but whether or not support was offered or money given, make it your priority to leave a meeting rejoicing over the opportunity of sharing your heart for the building of Jesus' kingdom. Presentations must be clear and visually effective. Asking people to endure boring missionary presentations is *not* productive! "Mission agencies have a terrible, beleaguered image. Their graphics, their terminology, their appearance is all out of an earlier era gone by. Their graphics are outdated. They don't catch the eye of the boomer." [13] ACMC can be helpful, as can media departments of mission agencies. Many have interesting materials available. When opportunity is given to make a presentation to a church or small Bible study, let the group feel your sense of

privilege in being a part of so great a job as missions. Yes, there is sacrifice, but I don't know any missionary who doesn't feel that to simply make money, pay bills and stand on the sidelines would be *more* of a sacrifice!

6. Consider ways to "network" with others of mission vision in the area. A missionary friend was able to bring four churches in Oregon together by meeting with the pastors and offering to *coordinate a missions conference* at which each church would have a role. Individually, none of the churches would have attempted such a venture. Together, they were able to invite a top missions speaker and share the logistical load to produce a meaningful missions event.

Prosperity Teaching

Another issue that affects missions-giving and affluence in the church is the "prosperity theology" popular with many North American congregations. A clear distinction must be made between "prosperity theology"and the biblical teaching regarding prosperity, for while the Old Testament promises spiritual *and* material abundance to those who obey God, it also warns of the dangers in accumulation of wealth and lack of concern for the poor (Mark 10:25, Deuteronomy 10:18, Isaiah 1:17, Jeremiah 22:3). Both the Old and New Testaments teach the importance of caring for the needy inside and outside the community of faith. The stress which many "prosperity" teachers place on obtaining personal blessing through faith *obscures* our responsibility to use material blessing for the glory of

God. Stress on material abundance can also cloud the scriptural admonition to receive suffering as an instrument in the sanctifying work of God. Historically, the church has viewed the suffering of the faithful from hardships such as the lack of finances, from persecution or disasters, as a *gift* rather than as *judgment*: "It is given us to suffer." This gift, Scripture says, should be received as an opportunity for intimate fellowship with Jesus and the continual process of His redemptive work on earth. Christians are to *share* in suffering, "filling up that which is still lacking in the afflictions of Christ" (Colossians 1:24). To teach that Christians should always experience comfort, wealth and success is *un*biblical, encourages a judgmental attitude toward those who are poor or suffer in other ways, and undermines responsible stewardship and missions activity in hard places.

Faith Missions—How does it work out in practice?

Consider this testimony and exhortation from George Müller, of Bristol orphanage fame, who was a strong influence in the "faith missions" movement:

> Over these years the Lord has faithfully taken care of us financially in our work of caring for the orphans by constantly raising up new supporters. God's promise is that they that trust in the Lord shall never be confounded! Some who have helped our work for a while are now with the Lord; others may grow cold in the service of the Lord and stop giving; others may desire to help but simply not have the financial means to do so;

others may have both a willing heart to help and
the means to do so but feel the Lord is guiding
them to be of assistance to another of His works;
thus for one reason or another were we to lean
upon man we would inevitably be disappointed;
but, in leaning upon the living God alone, moment
by moment, we are BEYOND disappointment, and
BEYOND being forsaken because of death, or of
not having enough to live on or enough love or
because of the needs of other works requiring support. How precious to have learned in any measure to stand with God alone in the world, and yet
to be happy and confident, and to know that no
good thing will He withhold to them who walk
uprightly! [14]

By standing with God alone, Müller did not
stand apart from involvement in the local church or
from its authority. His biography reveals a very heavy
commitment to the church in service, leadership and
finances. He simply wanted to bear witness that God
is a present, living, prayer-hearing God, and that it is
possible and practical to have a daily, intimate, walk
and active ministry with Him. Some feel that Müller
was able to accomplish all he did because he had a
distinct "gift of faith" that enabled him to walk and
work as he did. This was not his own assessment!

It is the selfsame faith which is found in
every believer. . . . Oh, I beseech you, do not think
me an extraordinary believer, having privileges
above others of God's dear children, which they
cannot have, nor look on my way of acting as something that would not do for other believers. . . . Do

but stand still in the hour of trial, and you will see the help of God if you trust in Him. [15]

The approach that Müller, Hudson Taylor, C.T. Studd and others of the historic faith missions took to raising funds is, of course, not the only biblical alternative. There are examples in Scripture of God's people requesting and receiving support. In the Old Testament, see 1 Kings 17:8–16 and Nehemiah 2:1–8. In the New Testament, Paul willingly received financial support from the churches. His letter to the church in Rome certainly infers that he was *asking* for support, and many evangelical agencies interpret Romans 15:24 in this way: "When I go to Spain I hope to have you assist me on my journey."

Dwight L. Moody laid a foundation for contemporary evangelical fund-raising. He had no difficulty presenting the financial needs of God's work to His people with "artless faith that all money belongs to the Lord, and that it can be had for the Lord's work if one goes about *in the right way* to get it." [16]

Individuals will find that their convictions and preferences regarding support-raising differ, and a certain approach may suit one but not another. A few essential principles must be kept in mind, however:

1. We must live and act in accordance with the biblical truth that God is our provider. His children need to exercise firm faith in Him and His promises to supply all our needs, both spiritual and material (Psalm 23:1; Matthew 6:33; 2 Corinthians 9:8; Philippians 4:19). Faith, then, should be preoccupied

with its object and not focus on the one who is exercising it.

Martin Luther wrote:

> Faith is only as strong as the one in whom we believe and trust. The efficacy of faith does not rest upon the intensity with which we believe, but in the reliability of the one in whom we believe. It is not the greatness of our faith but the greatness of God which counts.[17]

There are no human guarantees. Assurances from supporters may be given, but God alone can be counted on to "meet all our needs in Christ Jesus." We trust that the power of God is sufficient so that expansion and ministry outreach is not *controlled* by fixed budgets (though budgets may be useful guides) or by troubled economic forecasts, but rather by the promises of God in His Word (Hebrews 11 and 2 Peter 1:4). When individuals begin to look to the mission, friends, or supporting churches as the source of financial supply, disappointment and disillusionment will follow. The mission agency is only a channel used by God, who is the source.

2. Agencies have different policies on how and when missionaries may inform God's people of their needs, but all must strive to avoid manipulation to achieve financial gain. Solid biblical teaching on stewardship is needed in the church to the end that God's people are built up, rather than left confused and uncertain.

"Our desire is not that others might be relieved while you are hard pressed, but that there might be equality. At the present time your plenty will supply what they need, so that in turn their plenty will supply what you need." (2 Corinthians 8:13–15)

3. Integrity is required not only in the method of receiving monies, but also in how support money is used. Through embarrassing difficulties, the Christian church in America is learning the necessity for financial accountability.

St. Paul wrote: "We want to avoid criticism of the way we administer this liberal gift. For we are taking pains to do what is right, not only in the eyes of the Lord but also in the eyes of men" (2 Corinthians 8:20–21). May these challenging words of the world's greatest missionary be among our highest goals today.

CHAPTER SIX

Technology and Management by Objectives Is Doing the Job—Missionaries Stay Home?

"Christians now own more than 54 million computers. Electronic mail and 56 global computer networks now link the Body of Christ on nearly every continent. . . . Wycliffe Bible Translators, with the help of computerization, is now starting a new translation every 14 days, accomplishing in months translation tasks that used to take years."—Bill Stearns, author of *Catch the Vision 2000*, Bethany House

"Be careful with technology. Naturally I'm not advocating that we go back to the stone age. Technology is here to stay and must be placed at the service of missionary obedience. But it is mind-boggling to witness the level of technological sophistication at which the North American missionary undertaking has arrived. . . . Don't impose this type of computerized technology to the same extent on us. We do not have the resources necessary to keep up with that pace. . . . I fear that the information and communication war may be yet another form of paternalism. If you please, we want to relate to each other as people and as brothers and sisters."—Valdir Raul Steuernagel, Brazil, 1993 *Missions Handbook*

6

Genesis presents us with stories of the expulsion of man from Eden followed by the Tower of Babel—about limitations God placed on humanity. George Otis of the Sentinel Group suggests these limitations ". . .were not intended to permanently deny man access to creative knowledge but rather to slow his progress sufficiently so that wisdom would remain close at hand."[1] But it now appears that this creativity is reaching incredible proportions. Examples of the use of technological and management acumen abound in the secular world and in the realms of global evangelism and international ministry as well.

The results of the utilization of satellite television, on-line computer networks, virtual reality and digital technology are both thrilling and sobering. Several years ago, an American evangelist sponsored a worldwide communion service, which tied together a large congregation in Korea with 650,000 participants located throughout 180 American cities and 18 foreign cities. The Billy Graham Association has used this type of technology to reach many Asian and European cities with the gospel of Jesus Christ. Its latest application, in March 1995, was a technological extravaganza that transmitted the Graham Crusade from Puerto Rico to 165 countries.

A recent press release advertised a nationally televised concert of prayer patterned after an earlier broadcast which included 50 television stations, two national cable networks and nearly 300 radio stations. Churches across the nation are encouraged to invite other congregations in their community to gather together for prayer around a large-screen television or amplified radio signal.

Those committed to the unreached peoples task are grateful for computer services available: for example, the Global Missions Databank from the Association of Internationaal Mission Services (AIMS). The GMD provides a hub linking more than 20 databases. Surveys such as *Operation World* are also available for computer.

Discussion arises periodically among advocates of the World Christian movement concerning the application of strategy, planning, and technology in missions versus the spontaneous guidance of the Holy Spirit. In a missions class at a Philadelphia seminary, Dr. Harvie Conn referred to the contrast between the spontaneous work of the Holy Spirit in the early church and our modern tendency to highlight the need for cultural analysis, church and parachurch cooperation, and the use of hi-tech methods and equipment. He argued that we are becoming lopsided in our dependence on human means and planning strategies.

The discussion of human means versus spontaneity is not a new one. Both approaches have been advocated for years and both find supporters today. In the 1962 reprint of *The Spontaneous Expansion of the Church*, Roland Allen points out that the early church grew by the unorganized activity of individual members of the church explaining to others the gospel which had meant so much to them. He goes on to say that churches and mission agencies have lost the sense of conscious and deliberate reliance upon God in this day of highly organized missions. That was a generation ago. What would he say today?

In 1792, an impoverished youthful English pastor, part-time teacher and shoemaker, William Carey, wrote a small pamphlet urging upon the English church "An Enquiry into the Obligation of Christians to Use Means for the Conversion of the Heathens." Carey, considered by many the father of modern missions, exhorted himself and others to "expect great things from God [and] attempt great things for God." In style and purpose the "Enquiry" seems a forerunner to Patrick Johnstone's *Operation World*, with its charts detailing countries of the world, their sizes and populations, and the religions represented.

Carey argued that in light of God's promise to increase His kingdom, we who are joined to the Lord and made one with Him in Spirit ought to begin forming committees, making plans, and gathering monies for the propagation of the gospel. Of course, Carey had no inkling of the interfacing and cooperating possible in today's fax/computer/technology world. But an unbiased reading of his "Enquiry" suggests that he would approve of all these methods—or "means," to use his term.

Those who argue for more planning cite Carey and his promotion of thoughtful methods; others argue from a study of the New Testament Church for spontaneity, saying we ought to copy verbatim its approach to pioneer church planting.

Michael Green, a British scholar, takes a third position. He argues that though strategies will vary with time and culture, the necessary common factor is the fire of the Lord in the lives of His people. Following a study of evangelism in the New Testament, he says: "There does not seem to have been anything very remarkable in the strategy [of the early church]. . . . They had an unquenchable conviction that Jesus was the key to life and death, happiness and purpose, and they simply could not keep quiet about Him. The Spirit of Jesus within them drove them out into mission." [2]

Dayton and Fraser, in their book *Planning Strategies for World Evangelization,* discuss the use of hi-tech means to complete the task of worldwide evangelization, and comment, "Yet Jesus did use all the means at His disposal to relate the message of the kingdom of God to his target group. . . . It is not the specific form of early church methods that instructs us. It is the example they leave of spiritually empowered, faithfully motivated . . . communication of the good news." [3]

How do the Scriptures help us as we approach this question? In Luke 14:25–33, Jesus is speaking primarily about the cost of discipleship. By way of illustration He suggests the wisdom of assessing the task before us and moving accordingly. By using this illustration, He seems to suggest that a *lack* of concern for planning and results is inappropriate.

Two difficult Old Testament passages, 2 Samuel 24:1–17 and 1 Chronicles 21:1–17, are helpful in our understanding of the pitfalls associated with human plans and assessment. According to these passages, David, in order to assess his army and its ability to "get the job done," takes a census. David's concern for appraisal of his army meets with God's disapproval and judgment. Why judgment for simply taking a census? Does this taking of the census and assessing of his army demonstrate pride and security in human strength and equipment?

The passage and context of Zechariah 4:6, "Not by might nor by power, but by my Spirit, says the Lord Almighty," stresses the Lord's initiative and action in overthrowing anti-kingdom forces. Zerubbabel did not possess the army and power that David and Solomon enjoyed; nevertheless, God said He would rebuild the Temple and establish His kingdom through His enabling power at work in His people.

God has had to deal repeatedly with His people's tendency to rely on their own strength and independent means to accomplish His work. Many of us are happy to see 20th century technology used for the advancement of God's kingdom, but we also must recognize that throughout history God's power has been demonstrated through the crucified Lamb. Oswald Chambers reminds us that Jesus founded His kingdom on the weakest link of all—a Baby.

Management by objectives, organizational networking and electronic communications are valuable assets in the task of worldwide evangelization unless they deceive us into a false sense of human sufficiency. We must remain aware of the need to make intelligent application of the tools God is providing in our day in the context of Psalm 127:1: "Unless the Lord builds the house, its builders labor in vain."

Missionaries and pastors will find themselves wearied through well-intentioned efforts and the counsel of growth and business-management strategies if they attempt by these means to breathe life and numbers into churches that are struggling. G. Campbell Morgan contrasts this exhausting human effort with that of revivals such as visited Wales in 1904-1905:

> If you and I could stand above Wales, looking at it, you would see fire breaking out here and there, and yonder, and somewhere else, without any collusion or prearrangement. It is divine visitation in which God—let me say this reverently—in which God is saying to us, "See what *I* can do without the things you are depending on"; "See what *I* can do in answer to a praying people"; "See what *I* can do through the simplest who are ready to fall in line and depend wholly and absolutely upon *Me*." [4]

In a recent *World Pulse* article, Jim Reapsome, tongue in cheek, discussed the possibility of mission agencies following in the footsteps of a Japanese company directed by a Mr. Isao. Facing a shortage of young Japanese men willing to undergo the rigors of becoming Buddhist priests, Mr. Isao built a robotic Buddhist priest to perform the religious rituals required by his workers. Given the present decline in missionary applications, Reapsome muses:

> Just think for a moment about the possibilities. Shortage of missionaries? Send Robo Missionary. Cost of support too high? Send Robo Missionary. Can't adapt to the local climate and culture? Send Robo Missionary. . . . Taking too long

to raise your support? Send Robo Missionary. Sure, he costs $400,000. But raise it one time, and your deputation worries are over forever. . . . If we really want to reach the world by the year 2000, we don't have to worry about enlisting, training, and supporting missionaries. We just ask Mr. Isao to build as many missionaries as we need to finish the job. . . . There is one flaw in my plan: "Not by might nor by power, but by my Spirit," says the Lord Almighty. [5]

Are we to be primarily concerned with methodology and the attempt to become more efficient by using new technology and techniques? Or should we concentrate more upon praying for and laying the basis of Christian instruction for revival as it is described in the Bible, constantly laying our methodology open to scrutiny? Where do our dependencies lie? And can we reach a good balance?

"The spontaneous expansion of the Church reduced to its elements is a very simple thing. It asks for no elaborate organization, no large finances. . . . What is necessary is faith. What is needed is the kind of faith which, uniting a man to Christ, sets him on fire. Such a man can believe that others finding Christ will be set on fire also." [6]

CHAPTER SEVEN

Non-Westerners Are Doing the Job—Western Missionaries Stay Home?

"We rejoice that we are clearly entering a new era of partnership in Christian circles, not only in the West, but between the Western and non-Western world. The responsibility to evangelize is being taken up by the whole body of Christ."—Luis Bush and Lorry Lutz, *Partnering in Ministry, The Direction of World Evangelism*

"I believe that both the Western missionaries and the Third World missionaries will go to the final frontiers hand in hand, shoulder to shoulder. We need global missions from the global Church."—Thomas Wang, "Key Issues for World Evangelization," *International Journal of Frontier Missions*, November 1994

"Admittedly, there is great poverty in many countries, but teaching new churches to depend on Western resources can blind them to recognizing their own giving potential or seeking creative ways to overcome obstacles by trusting God."—Craig Ott, "Let the Buyer Beware," *Evangelical Missions Quarterly*, July 1993

"I am convinced that the Christian mission worthy of that name in the future is going to be truly international, ecumenical in the best sense of that term, unapologetically wholistic along biblical lines and daringly creative to face the brave new world order into which we are moving."—Samuel Escobar, "Mission in the New World Order," *Prism*

7

In this chapter we will discuss three aspects of the matter of cooperation in missions between the Western and non-Western world*: (1) providing money to finance non-Westerners in evangelism and church planting; (2) training and mentoring of non-Western missionaries and church workers; and (3) co-equal partnership arrangements between missionaries from the West and non-Western believers.

Send Dollars, Not People

Recently advertisements on behalf of the organization called Christian Aid have appeared in Christian periodicals proclaiming:

> There is no biblical basis for this tradition [of sending foreigners overseas to be missionaries]. It makes much more sense to help indigenous missions instead. Why send Americans at all? It's too expensive. A local Christian worker could do ten times more than the foreigner at 2 percent of the cost. It doesn't make sense. To all would-be

---

* A variety of terms is being used in this book, somewhat interchangeably, to describe non-Western peoples. Some authors prefer the term "developing world," others "two-thirds world" or "emerging world," and some simply the "third world." James Engel, in an unpublished paper, "The Reengineering of World Missions," says, "I am using the term 'third world' deliberately. I have found that those who live outside the West prefer these words rather than 'two-thirds world,' 'developing countries,' and so on." I too have found a variety of preferences on the part of Western and non-Western peoples.

foreign missionaries I say, "Get a job and earn all you can right here in the U.S.A.; then use your earnings to support a dozen native missionaries who are already on the field." —Dr. Robert Finley

The first and possibly strongest argument against the approach recommended by Dr. Finley is that it is impossible to reach an *unreached* ethnic group that way: there are no indigenous missionaries there to reach their own people. By definition, none of those people have yet believed, or else the believers are too few in number to have been mobilized for evangelism! Of course there *are* situations where local believers will prove to be best at evangelizing and shepherding both their own people and near neighbors—situations in which no learning of language or change of culture is necessary. But what about peoples who have neither local believers nor a strong enough nearby church to communicate a reproductive evangelistic model?

There is also the unfortunate fact of ethnic animosity to be considered:

Christian workers on their own rarely think about becoming missionaries to despised groups nearby. . . . [But] brothers and sisters in Christ from afar are often valued highly by local people because they are foreign, they are different, they know things about the rest of the world that are essential. They come with skills and knowledge which the people may not possess. [1]

In the case where no Christians are available among an unreached people group or its near neighbors, *someone* must go, necessitating a crossing of culture and language.

Sending money instead of people can be wasteful, even hazardous, and can provoke contention and greed:

> The Friends Missionary Prayer Band, with close to 1,000 missionaries, is being supported by some of the poorest populations in the world. . . . The FMPB will not accept a single cent from abroad. . . . Why? Because they value spiritual discipline more than money. They have prayerfully concluded that relying on foreign funds would spiritually damage their 30,000 prayer partners. [2]

Wade Coggins pleads that, "those who solicit involvement from North American Christians in the support of Third World missions should argue their case on its merits without calling for diminishing support for existing missionary efforts. In fact, such appeals would do well to reinforce the missionary vision now existing and call for expansion to greater partnership with emerging missions and the church around the world. New arrangements must be developed which create neither dependency nor paternalism." [3]

Warnings About Indiscriminate Distribution of Funds from the West

A 1993 *EMQ* (*Evangelical Missions Quarterly*) article by Craig Ott lists nine concerns about financially supporting national pastors and missionaries from the West:

1. Western support of national workers is a model that national churches cannot reproduce.

2. Such a strategy is based on the assumption that the spread of the gospel depends on money.

3. It can create dependency and stunt giving in national churches.

4. Heavy dependence on Western funds can reinforce feelings of inferiority.

5. Western support can create a mercenary spirit among nationals.

6. Workers paid by foreign funds are not always more effective and sometimes are even less effective and credible than lay workers.

7. It can rob the national church of the joy of being a truly missionary church.

8. Employing national missionaries may not be the bargain it appears. Many question whether national missionaries really live as cheaply as some claim, especially in the cities where the cost of living can be staggering.

9. Sending money instead of missionaries comes dangerously close to compromising the very essence of the Great Commission. The Great Commission calls us to not only send dollars, but ourselves. [4]

Ott concludes his article by quoting Wade Coggins on "the risks of sending our dollars only": "If our churches give only their money, and not their sons and daughters, our missionary vision will die in a generation or less. We can't substitute money for flesh and blood." [5]

Send trainers and mentors—not missionaries?

K. P. Yohannan, who was discipled and called into ministry through Operation Mobilization, in 1986 wrote a controversial book titled *The Coming Revolution in World Missions*. Yohannan is opposed to sending expensive missionaries from the West and is, instead, working to help facilitate Developing World Christians enter the mission field. Though he is not opposed to Westerners taking on some complex medical and community aid projects, he feels that village evangelism is best undertaken by locals or Two-Thirds World missionaries:

> Approximately 90 percent of all missionary finances are being used by 95 percent of the Western missionaries who are working among the established churches on the field—not for pioneer evangelism of the lost. From almost every perspective, then, it is obvious that mission spending is being done in areas far from the essence of what real Christian missions is about in the biblical context. . . . It is bad stewardship to send Western missionaries. At present the average American missionary family on the field is costing $43,000 a year, and inflation is increasing that cost every day. . . . In India, for only the cost of flying an American from New York to Bombay a native missionary already on the field can minister for years. [6]

Though mission agencies around the globe appreciate the fervor with which Yohannan has responded to God's calling of non-Western missionaries and agree with the need for appropriate allocation of funds, criticism of his book has arisen from a number of quarters. It can be summarized as follows:

1. Yohannan's argument is based on finding the *right* national to support. Following up on Craig Ott's

concerns, many examples exist of funds sent well-meaningly but undiscerningly from abroad which end up squandered, with no tangible results, corrupting local believers' motives, and/or simply being lost in the hands of unscrupulous administrators. The sending of checks calls for accountablity. More importantly, merely sending money from the West does not fulfill Jesus' command to the *whole* church to "go into all the world and preach the gospel." The appeal to "only send money" to support a national is really a pseudo-partnership and can form dangerous dependencies.

2. Most Western missionaries are now trained and sensitized to cultural differences and the need for a contextual approach to ministry. They have learned mission history lessons and are determined not to repeat mistakes of the past. Strategically they are prepared to apply biblical mission principles which have emerged during the course of history. Experienced missionaries on the field can readily enhance the effectiveness of newcomers and help them avoid mistakes made in the past. Frequently, new *indigenous* agencies find themselves reinventing the wheel in mission strategy and operations, and in the end find themselves leaning on established, experienced mission bodies.

3. In some situations, Western missionaries because they come into an area with no ancient ethnic enemies, are far *more* effective than locals or nearby people for whom centuries of conflict have created bitter rivalries nearly impossible to overcome, e.g., the Koreans and Japanese; the Muslims, Hindus and Sikhs of India; the Sunni and Shiite Muslims of the Middle East; the Hutus and Tutsis of Rwanda; the Serbs and

Bosnians, to name a few. As we see the increasing ful-fillment of Matthew 24—"nation rising against nation" (ethnic people group against ethnic people group)—outsiders who cross a number of cultural boundaries may be more welcome and able to minister than nearer, deeply distrusted neighbors. [7]

4. Many countries have tight social structures limiting meaningful contact between classes. A tremen-dous indigenous work of God is occuring in China at present, primarily among the rural peasants. The edu-cated class in the cities, however, pays little attention to their socially inferior countrymen. But foreign ex-perts and teachers have proven to be effective wit-nesses for Jesus in businesses and universities.

5. Though Yohannan acknowledges the need for Western Bible translation and medical services, does this do justice to the far-reaching consequences of Western inventiveness and perseverance in other ar-eas of gospel distribution?

Larry Poston, formerly a teacher with Greater Europe Mission, addresses Yohannan's challenge in his 1992 article, "Should the West Stop Sending Mission-aries?" and concludes:

> My native brothers and sisters preach the same gospel I do, and that gospel has always been "foolishness" and a "stumbling stone" to the lost. Native missionaries will carry their own cultural baggage and will be accused of religious imperi-alism. . . . Neither we nor they can win the world alone. We need each other. Let us join hands, en-courage one another, and put an end to the world's wait. [8]

Robertson McQuilkin, former president of Columbia Bible College (now Columbia International University), responds to the question "Why not let the nationals do it?" by saying,

> There are not enough "nationals," meaning non-Western missionaries, to finish the task. . . . Thrilling as the surge of "third world" missionaries is, and exhilarating as it is to contemplate that God may be by-passing the deficient Western church to get the job done, there are still not nearly enough cross-cultural pioneer church-starting evangelists from third world countries.[9]

McQuilkin also reminds us that it is biblically and theologically unsound to assign our responsibility to someone else:

> So long as there remains anyone on planet earth who has not heard with understanding the way to life in Christ, and so long as there is a community without a church, no congregation can stop reaching out and say, "It is finished; the task you have given us to do, we have accomplished."[10]

No doubt Yohannan and others present valid points for Western Christians to consider, particularly pertaining to how the West can facilitate the training of our non-Western brothers and sisters to be God's third wave of mission activity. Issues such as economic disbursement, however, call for serious attention and clear discernment. With large numbers of people groups still needing a gospel witness and active church, we should never eliminate the obligation of any part of the body of Christ to personally participate. Rather than predicating an either/or situation, *partnering in ministry* should be encouraged as an important trend and direction for world evangelization.

Partnership as Global Co-workers

Changes are taking place globally, providing a variety of models for partnership in missions, crossing language and cultural barriers.

Now *old* news, but still meaningful, is the fact that "a significant development in the history of the Church in our age is the rise of indigenous movements in Asia, Africa, and Latin America. . . . The winds of change blowing across Asia, Africa, and Latin America and the wind of the Holy Spirit moving upon the church in these continents indicate we are in an exciting period of mission history. . . . Third World missions have just made a beginning." [11]

We can rejoice when we see efforts to cooperate and to encourage nations which were once mission fields to become sending bases. Recently, Global Mapping International decided to make those involved in mission from the Two-Thirds World their highest priority. They feel that this is where most of the church resides today, and where there is tremendous potential for growth in spite of comparatively little access to technology and information.

Instead of emphasizing their differences and feeling threatened by other's strengths, we can rejoice that in the 1980s at least 368 Third World missionary societies were sending out a missionary force estimated at 13,000, and there has been continued growth. These new efforts are not being made without difficulty, and some of them offer exciting alternatives to the leader/ follower models of the past. In their book *Partnering in Mission*, Luis Bush and Lorry Lutz mention two major advantages of partnering:

1) Internationalization reflects the supracultural character of the gospel. As David Michell of OMF states: "We're going to live in heaven as one people. It's great here on earth to see what I think is the real ecumenical movement: those people of many different nationalities and church backgrounds who have a common conviction concerning the fundamentals of the faith." [12] I can say, "Amen!" In WEC International, we have found that the 46 nationalities working in our international missionary teams reflect the reality of the worldwide church.

2) Internationalization utilizes the complementary gifts of different peoples and cultures at the grassroots level.

It would seem that the internationalization of missions is a welcome fact of our time. In an unpublished paper, James Engel speaks of the "Reengineering of World Missions" and affirms the need for North Americans to take an enabling role with our Third World co-workers, defining the role as one of "demonstrating successful ministry making use of talents and gifts in challenging situations which require acceptance of diversity, mutual submission and integrity." [13] He goes on to say that "Not surprisingly, Christians in many countries such as Sri Lanka no longer welcome outside agencies or resource people unless they come alongside with a different spirit and intent."[14] Dr. Engel adds further that an important criterion for successful mentoring/partnership relationships is willingness to surrender our power over structures and resources.

We can be extremely grateful for the rise of the non-Western church. It is one of the most significant developments since modern missions began 200 years ago. However, this rise of Third Worlders does not lessen the responsibility of the Western church. It may suggest different strategies, and may alter our plans for pioneer locations. It may also speak to the spirit in which Western missionaries approach their non-Western co-workers.

William Taylor, director of the World Evangelical Fellowship's Mission Commission, says that when it comes to partnering issues, we must face *four hard questions*:

> *One,* how can the West stimulate non-Western missions without dominating them in terms of money, power, structures and initiative? *Two,* how can the West partner with sensitivity when the West subconsciously operates from a position of international leadership and initiative? *Three,* what kinds of partnerships does the non-Western world want, where they are seen as true equals and not merely cheap labor for effective cost-reduction and more 'bang for your buck'? *Four,* is the Western movement ready to serve as silent partners when the ravenous promotion machinery demands credit in order to generate more funds?"[15]

Ruth Stoik Anaya presented a paper to the faculty of Regent College titled "Cross-Cultural Friendship—Doing Theology Globally." Her concern is that missionaries have treated national co-workers as brothers/sisters in the formal religious sense but rarely embraced them as intimate friends, failing to overcome latent paternalism and racial prejudice.

> The concept of the universal church and the brotherhood of all believers is recognized and celebrated worldwide. . . . We accept and associate with anyone within this category, because they qualify by virtue of their Christianity. *But brotherhood stands aloof to the prized friendship relationship*—this being freely chosen (not consanguineal), highly personal (not categorical), and unconditionally loving (not commanded). Friendship has incredible potential for communicating love. Through friendship the Christian has unlimited opportunities to personify the truths of the gospel. Friendship crosses religious, race, class and language barriers. It is the language of love. It is the language of God Himself. [16]

Non-Western Missionaries—A Few Problems to Examine

In our rejoicing over the growth of non-Western missionaries we should bear in mind, however, that effectiveness in cross-cultural work is not exclusively the property of Third World workers. George Verwer, leader of Operation Mobilization (OM), reminds us that non-Westerners have no corner on cultural sensitivity. Multinational missions are presently facing this issue. At least two developing-country nations with growing churches have found that their missionaries can be very autocratic and insensitive to local cultures, with much to learn from Westerners about cross-cultural sensitivity. Winsomeness, cooperation, and servanthood in our witness are the fruit of our union with *Christ* and no one has a "corner" on these.

In the January 1995 issue of *Evangelical Missions Quarterly*, Stan Guthrie warns the Western church that there are some red flags showing up with the emerging non-Western missions movement. These are to be expected in a movement which has yet to mature. He quotes Alex Aroujo, an executive in International Operations of Partners International:

> It is very easy to idealize what we don't know much about, while our own well-known realities seem full of problems. The non-Western movement, though highly welcome and deserving of credit and encouragement, is a mixed bag of good and bad, of success and tragedy, and should not be idealized.[17]

In the same article, William Taylor of WEF is quoted as saying that participants of the 1993 Brazilian National Missions Congress "were stunned to hear that of the 5,400 missionaries sent out in the previous five years, the 'vast majority' returned within a year. Further, 90 percent of those returning early will not go back."[18] The reasons for this include lack of pre-field training and on-field pastoral support, poor strategizing, weak supervision and, of course, finances.

There is another consideration when we speak

of Westerners partnering and mentoring nationals of developing countries. Brian Woodford, who served for years in Burkina Faso, West Africa, and is now in an international leadership role in WEC International, finds it strange that while we criticize Western imperialism we fail to see the same spirit inherent in the suggestion that *we ought to put ourselves forward as mentoring experts.* Our ability to "enable," "mentor," or train non-Western Christians lies not only in our training and experience, but also in our knowledge of the particular culture and how application should be made to those we train. To be effective cross-culturally, mentors need to be learners first: of language, history, and cultural nuances. But whole blocks of our learning from Western seminaries, books, and seminars are "for Western use only." One size does not fit all. Certain church-growth principles may not apply across all cultures. We are not likely to be able to adequately discern what *does* apply and is relevant and what *doesn't* apply and isn't workable in a particular culture without the understanding that comes from spending an extended time *living* and *learning* there.

For example, church leaders from around the world have visited Bill Hybel's Willow Creek Church in Barrington, Illinois, to study church-growth principles. Valuable keys can be shared in such seminars, but much of the success Hybel's church has enjoyed is culturally bound and not suited for transplantation to other settings. Any attempt to export a particular model of Western church growth would obviously require the wise leadership of an experienced missionary/national team on the ground. A missionary mentor can fail to be effective and culturally relevant if no long-term overseas experience guides his or her "enabling" and mentoring.

Sound principles are necessary for fruitful, lasting partnerships. Phil Butler, the president of Interdev, has suggested the following:

1. Effective partnerships are built on trust, openness, and mutual concern.

2. Lasting partnerships need a facilitator or coordinator.

3. Effective partnerships have a partnerships "champion" inside every partner ministry.

4. Successful partnerships develop in order to accomplish a specific vision or task.

5. Effective partnerships have limited, achievable objectives in the beginning.

6. Effective partnerships start by identifying needs among the people being reached or served.

7. Partnerships are a process, not an event.

8. Effective partnerships are even more challenging to maintain than to start.

9. Effective partnerships are made up of partner ministries with clear identities and vision.

10. Effective partnerships acknowledge, even celebrate, the differences in their partner agencies' histories, vision, and services.

11. Effective partnerships serve at least four constituencies: the people they are trying to reach; the partner agencies with their own staffs and vision; the partner agencies' funding and praying constituencies; and eventually, the partnership itself with its growing expectations.

12. Effective partnerships have a high sense of participation and ownership.

13. Effective partnerships keep focused on their ultimate goals or vision and are not distracted by day-to-day operational demands.

14. Effective partnerships see prayer and communion as uniquely powerful elements to bind partners together in Christ.

15. Effective partnerships do not come free.

16. Effective partnerships expect problems and plan ahead for them. [19]

So what is our conclusion? The Great Commission is not yet fulfilled, and until it is, nationals and career and short-term Western missionaries need to join the fight with a willingness to learn and minister together with others from a variety of cultures—for training and for pioneer church-planting work.

CHAPTER EIGHT

Short-Termers Are Doing the Job—Missionaries Stay Home?

"In the Bible, stories tell how God used short-term missionaries to deliver His message. Some went on to become long-term missionaries. Others were called only for a specific project. God has been using short-term, cross-cultural workers for a long time. And He goes before His servants—just as He went before Jonah, the twelve apostles, the seventy-two disciples, and Philip—preparing hearts to receive His word."—Bob Sjogren, Frontiers

"It is difficult to imagine a compilation of the biographies, a century from now, of 'great short-termers' who advanced the cause of Christ in the late twentieth century."—Dr. Bob Coote, OSMC

"Some people still misunderstand short-term work. They can't discern between serious short-term programs where people are being stretched, trained and disciplined, and glorified overseas sightseeing trips."—George Verwer, OM

"Our goal in short-term missions is to build vision and motivate continued involvement. In no way does this contradict the words of missionary statesman Bishop Stephen Neil who stated 30 years ago that, 'We want missionaries who will lay their bones here.' We see short-term service as a strong potential stepping stone to this kind of sacrificial involvement."—James Engels, *Baby Boomers and the Future of World Evangelization*

"People are so anesthetized. There is so much apathy that something has to shock them back into reality. Short-term missions is that tool."—Rich Hurst, Missions Director, Crystal Cathedral

8

Some Thoughts on Short-Term Work

Some evangelicals, using Paul and his relatively short evangelistic visits to certain places as a model, suggest that the Great Commission will be accomplished by short-term missionaries. By "short-term" we mean not only young people who take evangelistic trips overseas but also teams that are involved in church-construction projects, in the training of nationals, in evangelistic campaigns, medical work, specialist projects, etc. And as we look at Paul's "patterns," it must be remembered that the entire world in which he worked could communicate in *one common language*, and the churches he established among pagan peoples ordinarily had also a large sprinkling of *God-fearers*— Gentiles who had a foundation in Old Testament teaching.

Experienced missionaries today are divided as to the value of short-term efforts. Though short-termers can be a potential asset in evangelism, can reinforce and refresh the ministry of the career missionary, can render valuable assistance in a great variety of practical projects, and may experience while abroad a confirmation of God's direction and call, they *do not* fulfill the long-term commitment required to accomplish most pioneering church-planting efforts. Language and cultural barriers are often a formidable challenge, requiring a *career* devotion to the task. Missionaries to resistant nations have found that obdurate walls blocking faith give way only under the sustained effort of long-term missionary service.

The Value of a Short-Term Experience

Unquestionably, the short-term mission option is here to stay, and for good reasons. Short-term mission ventures permit people of all ages and commitment levels to meet "real life" missionaries and national church leaders, which gives them a taste of a "slice of the world" outside their hometown. In light of the characteristic profiles of the Boomers/Busters and Generation X, short-term experience is perhaps the best way to enhance global vision among these generations. Many mission agencies have begun to welcome short-term workers, not as an end in itself but as an investment in the future—both for developing the fields and for growing a missions-mobilized church.

However, as the short-term phenomenon has exploded onto the missions scene, many career agencies have struggled with the need of reassigning field personnel from their basic ministries to that of overseeing and serving as translators/coordinators for short-term team activities. Reluctance to do this has been, in part, responsible for the origin of specifically short-term organizations. Other factors in the development of short-term agencies are more complex and technical, such as the determining of ministries and projects that particularly lend themselves to short-term participation. But increasingly, we can note with joy, field personnel have come to see that working with short-termers is an investment in people. Mission personnel frequently "pray the Lord of the harvest to send forth laborers"—and taking time to invest in short-termers can be a means of putting action behind prayer.

As previously mentioned, baby boomers and busters tend to make decisions on the basis of first-hand experience. They are willing to get involved through volunteer service, and in fact tend to make decisions and commitments based on knowledge gained *through experience.* Being personally acquainted with an experienced missionary significantly increases interest in a missionary career. Engel and Jones conclude: "Spreading the gospel overseas as a ministry is a high priority among those who have been on site overseas, those who are financial contributors to missions, and those engaged in personal evangelism."[1]

The Good News and Bad News of Short-Term Assignments

STEM Ministries (Short-Term Evangelical Missions) recently joined with Bethel College, St. Paul, personnel to evaluate the behavioral and attitudinal changes in those who have had short-term experiences. On all fronts, *positive* changes took place: prayer time for missions and missionaries significantly increased, missions giving doubled, mission-related activities increased by 64 percent (church-mission involvement, housing missionaries, mission-related education, etc.). Ninety-seven percent say their short-term experience strengthened and confirmed their commitment to world missions.[2]

According to Roger Peterson, the director of STEM, 32 percent of those who have done a short term with their organization have returned to the field, and the findings generally demonstrate an increase in participants' future contributions to the biblical mandate of world mission as a result of their short-term mission.[3]

These findings are heartening, but how are we to understand them in the light of Dr. Bob Coote's data that, in part, seem to be contradictory? Dr. Coote works at the Overseas Ministries Study Center and has written an article we referred to earlier in connection with career missionary statistics, published in the *International Bulletin of Missionary Research*, titled "Good News, Bad News: North American Protestant Overseas Personnel Statistics in Twenty-five Year Perspective." In his article he states that:

> Short-termers are a disappointment not only because they seem to number far less than we had imagined. Equally important is the fact that they have not had the effect of building up the career category by reenlisting in high numbers for career service after completing a short term overseas. To put it another way, the level of early resignations within the career group is such that conversion from short-term to career service has not been sufficient to make a substantial difference in career personnel totals. (It may also be said that without the conversion of short-termers to career status, the present level of career personnel would not be as high as it is.)[4]

The discrepancy between Coote's figures and Peterson's may be due to quality of preparation, experience on the field, and the adequacy or otherwise of the debriefing and follow-up the short-termer receives.

In our short-term program at WEC International, we have found that a thorough debriefing period and ongoing specific prayer *for* and correspondence *with* the short-termer are critical factors toward long-term commitment. If combined with practical training in cultural adaptation and proper debriefing, *short-term service can be fruitful and beneficial.*

Perhaps this is why agencies like OM and YWAM put academic preparation and practical ministry experience together in cross-cultural training programs for short-term work. My own short-term introduction to missionary work involved a college vacation spent in Mexico with OM, and then summers in Europe doing street evangelism with Christian Corps. We were constantly reminded of the importance of applying all three important elements of the training we were receiving: *knowing, being,* and *doing*—or academic preparation, spiritual formation, and practical ministry experience.

Retirees—An Untapped Short-Term Missions Resource

One short-term option is at present nearly untapped—the healthy retiree who wants to serve the Lord in missions. This group of people brings a maturity and breadth of experience which can benefit mission projects both here and abroad. From practical work to teaching, from houseparenting or house-grandparenting to computer consulting, retired persons can find a wonderful world of cross-cultural service. Understandably, this takes a measure of flexibility and the giving up of comfort and conveniences, but if there is a willingness to serve and a realization of the blessing unselfish service brings, opportunities abound! Many mission agencies welcome volunteer retirees, and several support agencies have been formed particularly to process retirees: SERVE (Sending Experienced Retired Volunteers Everywhere), HIM (Helps International Ministry), SOWERS (Servants on Wheels Ever Ready) and Golden Years Ministry. Information on these organizations can be obtained by contacting the author at the address and phone number in the back of this book.

Veteran Missionaries Speak their Mind About Short-Term

Argument as to the value of short-term experience as a confirmation instrument indicating suitability for *long-term service* comes from missionary veterans. In 1990 I conferred with field leaders and national church leaders from 57 different countries at an international missionary conference in Scotland. One of the topics we addressed was short-term workers. In general, the conferees affirmed many positive factors about short-term work which we have mentioned in this chapter: short-term service can be a mobilization tool, provide valuable respite for career workers, bring a fresh "spirit" of life and enthusiasm from outside, accomplish practical projects, bring expertise from mentors and specialist trainers, and foster a "World Christian" attitude in Western churches.

But seasoned missionaries do have some concerns. Dr. Mark Hinton, veteran of twelve years' work with national churches in East Africa, states that during his service in Kenya and his travels around Africa, he watched dozens of short-termers from the States come and go. Many short-termers arrive in a Third World country excited to be away from their homeland, brimming with enthusiasm to see, hear, touch, taste and smell everything about their host country. They've heard about culture shock, but upon arrival everything is wonderfully exciting and new, to be taken in and enjoyed. What culture shock? The people are all so friendly. Bonding seems to go well, the food is more palatable than they expected. Motivation is high. Skill and language levels may be low, but enthusiasm continues unabated and the camera is smoking. Before the emotional high subsides, they are back home, and the only thing that dampens their enthusisam is that not everyone seems to appreciate their stories or life-changing experiences.

On the contrary, for most new career missionaries the period of early cultural adaptation and language learning is daunting, at times discouraging, and often bewildering. Viewing the culture as a visitor is one thing; it is quite another to view it from the perspective that this will be your home indefinitely. The "honeymoon" quickly ends. What at first was interesting and different now seems noisy, filthy, and stupid. Not being understood or trusted undermines confidence; personal significance wanes when a person speaks and understands on a child's level. Does a three-week short-term experience begin to prepare a person for the stress of the long-term cultural onslaught? Many veterans say no. As in marriage, the realities of the new relationship do not begin to sink in until some time after the vows are made.

If a short-termer is more preoccupied with "vacation" than with the "purpose" of a short-term trip, he or she will never be sufficiently grounded in the place or people to understand what the "real thing" is like, any more than a couple would in a two-week "trial" marriage. Only unswerving commitment opens the door to deeper understanding of the real essence of missions. Dr. Hinton also expresses concern that we may be undermining the thrust for long-term workers by unwittingly communicating that a short-term experience is acceptable as an alternative to career service. This inference can leave short-termers with the satisfaction of having done their "bit" for missions and possibly erode any obligation to consider long-term commitment.

Another concern expressed by missionary veterans is that a national church can be worn out by constantly receiving short-termers. Incoming groups bring enthusiasm for experiencing everything. The church makes plans and adjustments to house, feed, entertain, and provide ministry experiences for the visitors, and then has to begin all over as one group leaves and the next one comes—each seemingly oblivious to the effort involved in hosting them. Imagine that kind of ebb and flow in our North American churches—the cry would go out for stability and commitment.

Unquestionably, short-term has become a fixture on the North American missions landscape. But is it really worth all the money and time? Robertson McQuilkin responds to the question this way:

> Unfortunately the proportion of short-termers who end up in career service is dropping from an earlier high of as many as 25 percent. More

careful promotion, preparation, and deployment is needed. When preparation—of the candidate and the field—is thorough, and when it is in line with realistic expectations, when the experience is in a place where things are happening, and when debriefing is a part of ongoing missions education, we can answer the question without hesitation, "Yes, short-term service is valid."[5]

Jim Reapsome adds that as the American church continues to "rev up" the short-term machine with the '90s-bent for speed and efficiency, "that same demand for speed seems to have permeated world missions activity, creating 'drive-thru' missionaries. According to the latest statistics, they far outnumber the ordinary, 'we're in it for life, so let's take time to soak up the culture and language' missionaries. . . . At the very least, we need to evaluate the results and implications of our mad dash for more drive-thru missionaries. The question is not 'Are they doing any good?' Of course they are. But immediate good results by themselves ought not to foreclose our search for some long-term consequences."[6]

There are practical steps that can increase the possibility of long-term mission consequences developing out of a short-term experience. One of these is the "debrief" session referred to earlier. But the returning short-termer *himself* also needs to evaluate his experience: "What impact has it had on me?" Perhaps *you* are a short-termer who is about to return home. Undoubtedly, contact with a different culture will have expanded your knowledge of the world. But has *God* revealed Himself to you in new ways? Then be ready to tell your story. Curious friends will be asking, "So how was your trip?" But don't be surprised if you sense a lack of empathy for the life-changing encounters you've had. Remember, they weren't there. Be patient; help them to understand by painting verbal pictures of those experiences without exaggeration or jargon. Focus on people you met; communicate lessons you've learned and emphasize the positive aspects of your trip. Also, avoid the understandable tendency to be critical of those in your home country who now seem to be extravagant and excessive in their spending compared to where you spent your summer. And begin now to take steps to shape a "world Christian" lifestyle for yourself. Look for opportunities such as the "Perspectives on the World Christian Movement" course to *deepen* your vision and perception of what God is doing in the world. Be careful to avoid debt, keep involved in ministry, and begin to develop lines of communications with agencies that can help you formulate a career missions plan if God is leading in that direction. Whether at home or abroad, work at integrating a *world vision* into your decision-making and church ministry.

A number of publications give practical guidelines for all aspects of short-term work, including the *Short-Term Mission Handbook, Stepping Out* and *The Great Commission Handbook,* all published by Berry Publishing, Evanston, Illinois. There is also YWAM's *Vacation with a Purpose.* And Michael J. Anthony has edited a helpful book titled *The Short-Term Missions Boom,* published by Baker Books in 1994.

A Parting Thought

George Walker, a missionary serving in Papua

New Guinea, relates the following story in "A Few Days' Sympathy." He speaks of a friend from his home church visiting the village where he and his wife were serving as missionaries, to get a firsthand look at the missionary activities of the Walkers. During his short stay the friend had a chance to meet several villagers. One man named Gabalame was a good friend of the Walkers and a dear believer.

> Our friend shared with Gabalame how he had been moved to sorrow as he observed the hard lot the Bisorio have in life. Our friend was challenged by both the physical and spiritual needs of the people of Papua New Guinea. As I translated for Gabalame what our friend had shared, he replied in simple, straightforward sincerity, "You have come for a few days and are moved. You have a 'few days' sympathy,' but are you moved enough to come back to Papua New Guinea for good and do God's work?"

> Gabalame's reply so stunned me that I was somewhat embarrassed to translate it back to my friend lest he think that Gabalame's comment was rude. The more I thought about it, the more it came to me that it wasn't a matter of Gabalame being rude, but of being honest. He was simply challenging our friend from the heart with the same issue that is on God's heart—the evangelization of those who have never heard.

> "You have a 'few days' sympathy.'" That stuck with me. In the long haul of doing the Lord's work it comes down to this—commitment. That's all that God desires—a total, simple yielding to Him to be used in His plan of reaching lost mankind.[7]

CHAPTER NINE

Tentmakers Are Doing the Job—
Missionaries Stay Home?

"We have ever held it be an essential principle in the conducting of missions that whenever it is practicable missionaries should support themselves in whole or in part through their own exertion."— William Carey

"As the Holy Spirit in Acts opened the door of faith to the Gentiles, even before the early Church considered it, so today potential self-supporting Christian missionaries are all around the world while many are not yet aware of what has happened. With mainland China, Russia and many Muslim nations opening more and more to this type of witness, may we today have ears to hear what the Spirit is saying to the churches."—J. Christy Wilson, Jr., *Today's Tentmakers*

"Even the premier tentmaker role today, teaching English, may not provide the teacher with enough time to actually start a church."—Robertson McQuilkin, *Evangelical Missions Quarterly*, July 1994

"Tentmaking has come to be thought of primarily as a financial strategy, and we don't think that it is. The issue is much more one of the people of God using the gifts of God . . . for the works of God."—Gary Ginter, *Christianity Today*, November 13, 1995

9

Some Thoughts on Tentmaking as an Alternate Missionary Option

"Tentmaking" here refers to the situation in which a Christian carries on secular employment in a cross-cultural setting (frequently in a restricted-access country), is recognized by members of the host culture as something other than a "religious professional," and yet, in terms of his or her commitment, calling, motivation and training, is a *missionary* in every way. The tentmaking approach of the last 15 years has "opened the eyes of expatriate Christians to the role they can play in achieving the Great Commission. Tentmaking consultants have been hammering out practical issues of motive, prayer and strategic support. Tentmaking should *not* be viewed as a means of avoiding raising support or an escape from spending the time and money necessary to become thoroughly trained in the Scriptures. Tentmakers should be such because God has called them *specifically* to that strategy for lighting a darkened corner" (Philippians 2:15). [1]

Tentmaking, originally seen as a peripheral missionary endeavor, has gone "mainstream" through conferences such as Glorietta II, held in September 1994. "We wanted to get away from theoretical discussions and processes and instead talk about successful tentmaker models that really work," says Cliff

Westergren, who has been managing tentmakers with the Christian and Missionary Alliance. [2]

Changes in thinking about tentmaking, as well as political and economic realities, have helped to clarify the varying roles of tentmakers. Typically the tentmaker works in "RANs" (Restricted Access Nations), where visas are difficult to obtain. At least three different tentmaking approaches can be distinguished.

1. *Short-term*: The tentmaker may obtain a job overseas, usually contractual and temporary in nature. This short-term tentmaker is a witness in his or her job, but does not ordinarily attain significant language or cultural skills.

2. *Long-term*: A tentmaker with a longer commitment holds a job in the country and additionally makes every effort to gain language and cultural skills and become a partner in local church-planting strategies. (English teachers and foreign business experts might fall into either of these two categories.)

3. *Entrepreneural*: A third group of tentmakers is concerned about the extensive time and commitment required by a vocational contract. Ordinarily, therefore, these tentmakers attempt to set up a business that gives access to visas and local credibility, yet offers flexibility, allowing priority to be given to evangelism and church planting.

An excellent resource for further examination of tentmaking is Jonathan Lewis's *Working Your Way to the Nations: A Guide to Effective Tentmaking*, published by William Carey Library.

Organizations such as Intent, located in Cascade, Colorado, serve the church and tentmakers. Intent is a volunteer service organization, combining the experience and expertise of practioners, enablers, and sending organizations seeking to share their experience so as to facilitate the recruiting, equipping, and support of tentmakers worldwide.

A Few Cautions for the Tentmaker

Lest we think that tentmaking is *the* answer to world evangelization, we must consider a few matters.

1. In many places language skill is required for effectiveness in evangelistic or church-planting ministry. Tentmakers should not have "illusions of grandeur" about what can be accomplished without mastering the language and making a long-term commitment to the people. Many mission agencies require an established language-skill level before the tentmaker actually begins working at a job in the country. Without some level of fluency in the national language, English speakers there tend to flock together, distancing themselves from the nationals and short-circuiting effective personal evangelism and church-planting ministry.

2. Many tentmakers are finding they need a greater depth of biblical knowledge than previously thought. Though a seminary degree is not necessary, inquiries and problems will arise that require at least a foundational level of biblical or theological training.

3. It is difficult to live in another culture, work full time, and do church-planting work. "Even the pre-

mier tentmaker role today, teaching English, may not provide the teacher with enough time to actually start a church."[3] Some agencies are suggesting that field missionaries work in cooperation with the prospective tentmaker to find him a job that does not require a full 40-plus-hour work commitment—so that language and culture learning is not just a "tack-on" effort. Speaking from six years of tentmaking experience in Europe, I remember the great ministry intentions I had—only to discover that the majority of my time was spent in learning how to adequately function at my job in a new culture! Though there was some meaningful evangelism in those years that related directly to those I worked with, much of my energy was dissipated in responsibly satisfying my employer. Frequently I went to my evening or weekend discipleship and evangelistic ministry feeling *spent* emotionally and physically. Ministry did not receive my best efforts; my day job did! Though some fruitful evangelistic efforts did occur—for we attempted to bring together the fruits of our labor into a living body of believers—that time-and-energy-consuming church-planting ministry received only our "second best" effort.

4. Many unreached areas of the world do not have the economic structure to accommodate tentmakers. As the Personnel (Candidate) Director for our mission, I was once approached by a medical doctor who was interested in working as a tentmaker among a specific unreached ethnic group in one of the poorer nations of West Africa. Unfortunately, there was no way any agency or organization, much less that particular country, could *pay* him to do medical work and evangelism. He had heard about the option of doing

missionary-related activity while receiving a salary through a tent-making job and, wanting to avoid the effort of support-raising, had set his hopes on going to Africa in this manner. He was disappointed to learn that tentmaking is neither appropriate nor viable in many developing, economically struggling nations.

5. Some tentmakers have difficulty with what appears to be "deception" regarding their status. Ultimately they are in the country for *spiritual* reasons, but must give the appearance of a professional "front." Not everyone finds this a problem, but those who struggle with it must find resolution or seek another ministry niche. People who have already sorted through this problem may be of great assistance to them.

Tentmaking *is* a valid addition to the missionary enterprise, providing legal entry into many RANs (Restricted Access Nations). But tentmaking must be approached with the same serious preparation as the classic missionary vocation would be, not as a "fast-track" route to missions. The prospective tentmaker needs discipling and training to become an effective cross-cultural witness and church planter. And after arriving in his or her host country, the tentmaker needs to be plugged into a supportive network for prayer and strategy. Struggling in isolation seldom succeeds for long, and has been the catalyst for sending tentmakers home early, wondering that they did *not* fulfill their goal of being a witness for Jesus.

CHAPTER TEN

Encouraging Trends in Missions Today

"Evangelical Christians are the fastest growing major religious group in the world today and it is the only one that is growing rapidly by conversion."—Patrick Johnstone, author of *Operation World*; reported at GCOWE (Global Consultation on World Evangelization), 1995

"He who has inspired His people to pray kingdom-sized prayers will not fail to answer us."—David Bryant, Concerts of Prayer International

"In Kenya . . . we had learned that life does not consist in an abundance of possessions, that God's glory can be demonstrated without flawless managerial skill, that people are splendid and brimful of personality under very awkward circumstances. We had found something surprising in the Kenyan air: a sense of humor. I wanted my children to know something about that liveliness and humor."—Tim Stafford, "Finding Hope in Africa," *Christianity Today*, July 17, 1995

10

As we consider difficulties and challenges in the mission task I want to suggest a few encouraging global trends in missions:

1. North American Christians are opening their homes to immigrants and students from abroad. Great opportunities and freedom for ministry abound with students from restricted access countries who have moved into our neighborhoods. We have an incredible opportunity to touch the frontiers of many countries through students and international visitors from places like the Middle East and China. Stanley Haeuerwas and William H. Willimon have written *Resident Aliens* (Abingdon Press, 1989) to aid Americans in being effective witnesses in their own nation.

2. There is the growing influence of organizations like ACMC (Advancing Churches in Missions Commitment), which is an agency existing to mobilize Christian congregations for effective involvement in world evangelization. ACMC provides resources to equip church leaders, creates opportunities for congregations to stimulate one another to excellence in missions ministry, and links churches with other missions resources.

3. Global prayer groups and movements are springing up. Groups such as the AD 2000 United Prayer Movement and Adopt-a-People report that focusing prayer on 62 nations has resulted in some exciting breakthroughs. Other movements of prayer are

specifically targeting large urban centers and the 10/40 window. These groups include: Campus Crusade's World Prayer Crusade, Christ for the City, Concerts of Prayer, Discipling a Whole Nation, End-Time Handmaidens, Esther Network, Every Home for Christ, Generals of Intercession, Intercessors International, Lausanne Global Prayer Strategy, Lydia Fellowship, March for Jesus, Prayer Support Networks, Southern Baptist Bold Mission Thrust, Women Aglow, and YWAM Cardinal Points. "Prayer has dramatically changed the face of the globe as 25 percent of the countries of the world have changed governments in the past two years. The massive prayer unleashed by this united effort is bound to be a major factor in the continued acceleration of God's global purpose." [1]

The sheer number of spontaneous prayer efforts and movements suggests that they may be a precursor to a move of God's Spirit. These prayer movements take on special significance—for historians will remember that it was at Williams College, Williamstown, Massachusetts, during a revival in 1805-1808, that Samuel John Mills (1783-1818) and his friends committed themselves to the work of foreign missions in the now famous "haystack prayer meeting." For several years thereafter, many students, having experienced personal revival, offered themselves for evangelism on the frontiers of mission work in what later came to be known as the "Student Missionary Uprising."

Remembering great movements of God in mission history and learning from them is not to enthrone the past but to learn from it! The key to church renewal, Donald Bloesch says, does not lie simply in returning to the confessions and experiences of past ages. "The Holy Spirit always speaks a new word to his people, a word that does not negate the words he has spoken in the past but clarifies and fulfills the partial illuminations already given." [2]

The Student Volunteer Movement for Foreign Missions, back in the 1890s, stressed practical holiness and empowering for service together with active strategic ministry. The Student Volunteers were exhorted not only concerning the needs of the world but also regarding the needs of their hearts in "Preparation for Christian Service." The Rev. F.B. Meyer used that as the title of one of his messages. In it he recounts the story of a young C.T. Studd—in which "Charlie" testifies to yielding his whole life to the Lord, thereby removing those elements which had distracted him and were causing him to swerve off course. Studd told F.B. Meyer, "Why, what a fool I was! God wanted to take away the sham jewels to give me the *real* ones. He took away the thing which was eating out my life and instead gave me *Himself*!"[3] Stories of consecration like this, leading to a life of fruitful service, are the fruit of prayer movements such as we see bursting forth around the globe even today.

4. There is a growing expectation about the coming years of pioneer missionary venture and the endeavor to evangelize the remaining unreached peoples of the world. Although most Christians are not prepared to be dogmatic about the year 2000, there is mounting evidence that with continued missionary vision *this* generation could complete the Great Commission. Patrick Johnstone, author of *Operation World*,

has predicted that if present trends continue, the final unreached peoples could be reached near the turn of the century. Missionary visionary Ralph Winter contends that "never before have the stakes been so high or the opportunity so great. Never before has it been so impellingly possible for us to give our utmost for his highest." [4]

Luis Bush agrees with these forecasters: "Several factors today renew the sense that world evangelization is possible: 1) Divinely initiated breakthroughs like the one in the Marxist world. It's harvest time. 2) Increasing prayer mobilization among God's people. 3) Participation of people from different ethnic backgrounds. 4) Spiritual initiatives around the world toward the year 2000." [5]

5. A welcome aid in this quest to reach the remaining unreached peoples is the clarification of the task provided by individuals and organizations such as Ralph Winter, the Adopt-a-People Clearing House, Patrick Johnstone and David Barrett. Patrick Johnstone, in addition to serving as Research Director for WEC International, also chairs the Unreached Peoples Network for the AD 2000 & Beyond Movement, which met from November 28 through December 3, 1994, to decide on a publishable list of the remaining unreached ethnic groups on earth. Out of this and subsequent discussions, Mr. Johnstone developed a dramatic new concept for defining the remaining task of world evangelism—targeting "affinity blocs" of peoples as gateways to the remaining unreached. He states:

> During my sabbatical in the last five months of 1993, I had the privilege of spending

three months in Richmond, Virginia, with David Barrett and his research team. This, to me, was a seminal time in that insights gained and researches done have molded much of my research and public ministry since. For years, one of the key issues for world evangelization has been the challenge of Unreached Peoples. How many are there and where are they? These questions are crucial for the completion of the Great Commission that Jesus gave us. Yet for years we researchers have floundered in the complexity in our efforts to define and analyze the global picture. The rough consensus beginning to emerge is that there are about 12,000 peoples in the nations of the world, and about 2,500-3000 of these would possibly still represent a pioneer missions task. Yet that number is hard to grasp, so nearly all of these less-reached peoples can be grouped as follows:

a. Of the 2,500 peoples or "nations" that have less than 2 percent Christians, 1,600 belong to seven large families of peoples with related languages or cultures.

b. Another 130 Gateway Peoples—hub peoples for possibly 80 percent of all the least-reached peoples—can be identified.

These concepts have become a powerful tool for making the unfinished task more intelligible, mobilizing prayer, forming missions partnerships and strategic targeting.[6]

Grouping unreached peoples in affinity blocs makes the concept much easier to grasp. As gateways to the remaining unreached, we must reach the Sahel peoples of Africa, the Arabs, the Turkic peoples, the Iranian-related peoples, the Malays, the North Indian and the Tibeto-Burman peoples, plus 330 peoples unrelated to these seven affinity blocs. Patrick Johnstone warns, though, that "we may over-simplify the task, fail to cooperate adequately, and underestimate the human, spiritual and financial cost involved in this stupendous task." [7]

6. Another of the encouraging "signs of the times" is the reconciliatory and partnership ministry of groups like WEF (World Evangelical Fellowship). This international movement brings together Christians from a variety of cultural and church backgrounds, providing a platform for the Church universal to interact, meet, pray for, challenge and encourage one another, as well as to mobilize to finish the task. In these days of the "global village," an international, interdenominational movement like WEF can help Christians around the world work together on our common goal: to proclaim the gospel to all peoples.

Recently, friends told me about their participation in a weekend "Promise Keepers" rally. This movement challenging men to godliness and faithfulness is sweeping the U.S., producing repentance and new life in men of all ages and races, from many denominations and socio-economic backgrounds. One of the "commitments" pledged by a "Promise Keeper" is that he will "Influence the world by being obedient to the Great Commandment (Mark 12:30–31) and the Great Commission (Matt. 28:19–20)." Can we hope that the enthusiasm and spark coming from this move of God will cause *men* to set aside career agendas, offer themselves for mission service, and join the multitudes of *women* who have so faithfully responded to God's call over the years?

CHAPTER ELEVEN

What Next?

"People feel as if the hand of God were turning a page in human fate. We have a sense of things ending and others beginning."—Henry Grunwald, *Time*, March 30, 1992

"Missions is not the goal of the church. Worship is. Missions exists because worship doesn't."—John Piper, *Let the Nations Be Glad: The Supremacy of God in Missions*

"The great hunger is on me more than ever for Him and His work. O how few love Him and how feeble is my most passionate love. I scarcely know anyone who is consumed for Him. It is all creeds and phrases and belief, but for Him how few! To know Him—that is it."—Oswald Chambers

"The purpose of world missions is the glory of God. 'Declare His glory among the nations, His marvelous deeds among all peoples' (Psalm 96:3). Christian missionary work is the most difficult thing in the world. It is surprising that it should ever have been attempted."—Stephen Neill, *Call to Missions*

"Ah, Lord God! You have made the heavens and the earth by your great power and stretched out arm. There is nothing too hard for you."—Jeremiah 32:17

11

The statistics we have analyzed demonstrate a decline in the North American career missionary force in a day when opportunities for mission work abound. In response to the present situation worldwide, representatives of the AD 2000 & Beyond Movement have called for thousands of new missionaries from the United States. Wycliffe Bible Translators has put out an urgent request for Bible translators, saying at least as many more language groups need translations as have been dealt with up till now. Agencies such as SIM International tell us "It takes a tough Christian to be a missionary," challenging Christians to service around the globe. CLC has put out a plea for 100 new missionaries and TEAM invites young people to "Grow while you serve overseas." Patrick Johnstone of WEC International has recently identified "gateway peoples" through whom impact for the gospel will have great significance. This is just the beginning of a long list of agencies, both denominational and interdenominational, with experienced mission track records, not to mention newer groups, all looking for Christians who want to have an impact on the world for whom Jesus died.

To be biblical we must understand that redemption and global outreach originate in the heart of God; the Great Commission is a divine imperative, not a reflection of cultural imperialism. People are lost without Jesus Christ, the only mediator between God and

mankind (1 Tim. 2:5) and the only source of true salvation (Acts 4:12; John 14:6). As Christians, our mission and our privilege is to declare Jesus to a lost world,
to every people, tribe, tongue, and nation on the earth.
God has sovereignly chosen to change and redeem the
people on this planet through *us*, His Church.

In American society, the generation of people
currently entering adult maturity have come of age in
a cultural and moral "whirlwind of barbarism." However, some characteristics for which these Baby
Boomers/Busters and Generation X'ers have received
bad press are the very qualities that could enable them
to be effective as pioneer missionaries: "Their pragmatism and skepticism, their sharp-eyed assessments
of life and, above all, their search for community and
personal relationships are exactly what the emerging
era requires."[1]

Obedience to the Great Commission here and
abroad is one of the keys to sustaining the fire of God
in our lives. In an article titled "How Can We Reach
Generation X?", Ron Luce says, "This generation is
waiting for us to challenge them with a purpose worth
living for and a cause worth dying for. And they're
waiting for us to show them, not just tell them, what
to do."[2] Is a William Carey, an Amy Carmichael, a
Hudson Taylor, or a C.T. Studd out there somewhere?

Recently a friend was discussing with the president of a Christian college plans for a short-term missions trip to the Middle East. The college president remarked on how appropriate it is in these days that
North Americans are going only for short stints and
are allowing the nationals to do the long-term work

required overseas. Christians who have accepted this thinking need to be educated to realize that pioneers from the West are *still* needed to work among unreached peoples in evangelism and church planting. To be sure, the Western pioneer may often be partnered with or working under a national co-worker or church. But it should not be overlooked that in many places these do not even exist, and traditional career missionaries are still required to "boldly go where no man [missionary] has gone before."

While teaching at the Missionary Training College (MTC) in Tasmania, Australia, my wife and I became acquainted with two students, Richard and Evelyn Hibbert. Both had training as medical doctors but believed that God was guiding them to cross-cultural work in the areas of evangelism, discipleship, and church planting. Missionary service in Kardzali, Bulgaria, followed training. Evelyn has written an article for *World Pulse* concerning a move of God among the Millet (pronounced "mi-LET") of Bulgaria:

> Rapid growth, illiteracy, and the imbalance of women missionaries to men have created a leadership and discipleship crisis. . . . There is a dearth of workers (national or foreign) and resources to help. Since 1990 short-term workers have flocked to Bulgaria, many of them attracted by the opportunity to work with Muslims in a free environment. Some good has been done, and some harm. The strain has been great on some Millet and Turkish pastors, as well as the very few resident foreign workers. *The need, however, is for people who will stay for 10 to 20 years, learn Turkish well, and live among the Millet and Turks. Those who do, gain credibility in*

ministry and provide a model in lifestyle (especially as Christian families). Some Millet are becoming missionaries to the Turkic world, despite the difficulties.[3]

I find in Evelyn's article a repetition of Patrick Johnstone's plea for a new generation of career missionaries who bring with them a willingness to invest their lives in a people and a committment to language and culture preparation necessary to *see the job through.*

Statements like the following, in which research by Dr. James Engel is evaluated, are painful to those of us who work in traditional missions:

> His preliminary findings are that traditional missions are a dying entity. He describes North American mission boards as generally static or experiencing financial shortfalls. Engel says, "If this trend is perpetuated, North America cannot support efforts to meet needs worldwide." His research documents a massive decline in impact of North America on the world Christian scene. Engel attributes this trend to what he calls the "Fortress Mentality" of the North American church, which focuses on fighting domestic issues and legal cases rather than preaching the gospel. As he sees it, the church is dealing with symptoms, not problems, both here and abroad. He contends that the only way to reverse this trend is to break out of the traditional mission mindset and live the gospel.[4]

What recommendations can we make? In light of misunderstandings and confusion about the real need for career missionaries from North America, and in order to deal with issues often seen as barriers to missionary service, the following are suggested:

1. There must be an increase in sound teaching concerning the biblical mandate for missions and about the condition of those who die apart from Christ. Scriptural teaching on "who believers are in Christ," their authority in Him and their New Testament calling, is *imperative*. (Colossians 2:9–10 declares: "For in Christ all the fullness of the Diety lives in bodily form, and you have been given fullness in Christ, who is the head over every power and authority.") Local church teaching can be supplemented by such ministries as the "Perspectives on the World Christian Movement" course, ACMC conferences, and other conferences and information offered by mission agencies and parachurch organizations for deepening mission awareness, spiritual life, enthusiasm leading to mobilization, and commitment.

2. We must emphasize the need for appropriate preparation for the task. The complexity of the world and the reality of the evil spiritual forces working to undermine missionary efforts call for well-prepared heads and hearts. Willingness and dedication are truly necessary, but to them must be added understanding, skills, and perseverance. This is not an argument that lengthy seminary degrees are essential preparation for missionary service, except perhaps when a teaching ministry is planned. However, every missionary will be a Bible teacher on some level, even if only one-on-one, and so must have a solid core of Bible training. Thankfully, practical missions training including cross-cultural issues is available through, for

example, Bethany Fellowship, the U.S. Center for World Missions, WEF, Columbia International University, Missionary Internship, WEC International's "Gateway" Training Center in Vancouver, Canada, and programs of various lengths at many colleges and graduate schools throughout the U.S. and Canada. The key is to make missionary training applicable, practical, and "hands-on," rather than abstract, theoretical, and intellectual. Missionary training in our complex world must also be *international*—not given from a purely American viewpoint or relevant only in an American context. Texts such as David Harley's *Preparing to Serve: Training for Cross-Cultural Mission* (William Carey Library) and William Taylor's *Internationalizing Missionary Training* (Baker) assist those involved in developing culturally appropriate missionary training programs.

3. A crucial characteristic for any aspiring missionary applicant is willingness to listen, to learn, to experiment with new roles and responsibilities, and to recognize the gifts and abilities of others. Churches have the basic responsibility to disciple members toward the servanthood roles that need filling on the mission field and in working with and under those of other nationalities.

4. Mission agencies are constantly reevaluating strategy in light of the political and social changes occuring around the globe. One area being given much thought and study is that of families and their children's educational needs. While working toward the best interests of families, the mission community pleads with the church in the West to reevaluate its

uninformed, "knee jerk" reactions to methods of MK education, particularly boarding schools. Many agencies make provision for a wide range of educational alternatives including home schooling, local day schools, tutors, national and international schools, as well as MK day and boarding schools. Parents considering missions should speak to various agencies to determine what facilities and options are available.

Anyone interested in children in missions should bear in mind that the myth of MKs being inevitably emotionally damaged has been wildly overstated. Certainly, some MKs have problems, but how does this compare with the number of children who grow up in churches and "safe" Christian families in America, yet develop problems? I recall hearing Floyd McClung, leader of YWAM, respond to an inquiry at the Urbana missionary conference. At the time, the McClung family was living in the "red light" district of Amsterdam, Holland. When questioned about the dangers of raising a family in that setting, Floyd stated strongly that he and his wife felt their children were far safer spiritually where God had placed them, in a community filled with drug dealers, alcoholics and prostitutes, than they would have been facing the subtle but pervasive effects of sin in American society. The clear consequences of sin in their neighbors gave the McClung children an object lesson the parents knew would never be forgotten.

5. Reactions to the value of short-term missions differ widely. Unquestionably short-term has become ingrained in the American evangelical church framework. The learning trend of this generation is satis-

fied by short-term experience. Short-term experience *can* yield positive results for missions in the long run. Yet those on the mission field give the subject a mixed review. Field leaders and national churches usually do recognize the long-term investment being made by working in the present with short-termers. However, career workers also struggle with having to set aside their ministries and responsibilities to oversee "Christian tourism."

Short-term teams need to be carefully prepared and trained to maximize their short-term experience. Cross-cultural sensitivity, team and interpersonal dynamics and conflict resolution, spiritual disciplines— how to feed from God's Word while away from the fellowship at home and how to have an effective prayer life—all these elements are essential. A few weekends spent together as a team before departure, with discussion and training on the above topics, can make a great difference. Pastoral staff should always be involved in the trip. Short-term organizers should carefully screen applicants and be prepared to ask any to stay home until minimal criteria are met regarding spiritual maturity. Blocks of time should be set aside for team prayer for the host nation and its people. Ideal projects enable short-termers to help in practical work situations *and* build relationships with nationals. Taking steps out of one's own cultural comfort zone can revolutionize a person's perspective. Short-term service should be seen not as "fulfilling a person's missions requirement" but as the beginning of lifetime "Great Commission" involvement.

6. Several years ago I received a call from a veteran missionary who, with his family, had served a

number of years in Africa. He wanted to inquire as to our organization's missionary-support levels. His problem, he related, was that while he and his family were on furlough, his mission board had raised their support requirement to such a level that he did not feel, in good conscience, that he could approach churches and other supporters. He felt stuck.

We must heed issues like this and others that Jon Bonk raises in his book *Missions and Money—The Problem of Western Missionary Affluence.* Not only are North American churches increasingly unsympathetic to the mission cause as expenses rise, but problems exist in some places overseas where affluence undermines our message.

7. The fact that, according to Larry Pate in his study *From Every People,* there are well over 1,100 non-Western mission agencies, increasing in number every year, is cause for rejoicing! Under the leadership of people like Dr. Chris Marantika, founder and president of the Evangelical Theological Seminary of Indonesia, new models of partnership are developing to "pray together, pay together and proclaim together." Rather than replacing the Western missionary, working together as partners who mutually benefit from what each brings to the task is the way toward the common goal of seeing God's kingdom extended.

Great wisdom and discernment must be exercised in giving the non-Western missionary financial support from the West. Experience suggests that capital investments might be wiser than support for individuals. William Taylor, Director of the Missions Commission of the World Evangelical Fellowship, says:

Because I move among the non-Western missionary movement and try to be sensitive to its needs, I have struggled with these issues. But let me quote an Indian missions leader who told me some years ago: "If Americans want to send funds to non-Western missionaries, that may be fine in some cases. But do not rob us of the joy and responsibility to support our own people. And I fear that if Americans send now only their dollars and not their sons and daughters, the next step will be to send neither their dollars nor their sons and daughters. There is a nonbiblical extreme to be wary of. Biblical partnership means sending and supporting your own flesh and blood." This was wise. It is not a matter of either-or, but both-and.

Another Asian missions leader told me, "A lot of Asians are raising funds in the U.S. Please tell your colleagues there to check with respected nationals in our countries who can vouch for the integrity of these ministries. Tell Americans to be careful." [5]

8. Tentmakers will continue to find opportunities to work overseas and begin businesses with proper funding and technical expertise. Being able to spend time immersed in language and culture learning is one key to fruitful service as a tentmaking missionary. Another is being linked with a praying, strategizing team on the field. Trying to work as a "lone ranger" too often results in bewildering discouragement and an early trip home.

9. The information/technology superhighway can be an avenue of opportunity and efficiency. Electronic mail has taken the mission world by storm. Our

agency has found e-mail's low cost and speed extremely helpful in a day when speedy communication is vital. The Christian Interactive Network, available on Compuserve, recently wrote about a computer fiber-optic network for China. Many of my mission friends use their PC link with friends and supporters via e-mail to send "prayer letters." Portable video equipment and generators are utilized around the globe in urban and rural settings to show evangelistic movies like the "Jesus film." Wycliffe Bible Translators are working on a technology called Lingualinks which will help in each phase of translation work—anthropology, computing, translation, socio-linguistics, literacy, and language learning—and will significantly speed up the work of translation.

Each of these technologies requires praying, sacrificing workers who are willing to commit their lives to its implementation. Support tools are ready for use by Christians who may not realize their technical skills can be used for God's kingdom. God has provided technology to accomplish some of the administrative drudge-work of missions and free up more people to engage in evangelism and church planting.

9. Lastly, the importance of spirtual formation in ministry training cannot be overstated. As mentioned in a previous paragraph, the development of both the mind and the heart is critical in preparing the aspiring missionary. Books and seminars today tend to separate ministry objectives and strategies from experiential holiness and spiritual equipping. We hear of one or the other, but they are not often presented as

intrinsically linked. As churches and mission boards assess candidates for mission service, both academic and technical qualifications *and* spiritual formation and maturity need to be considered.

The national church on the field holds high expectations regarding the vocational gifting *and spiritual life* of the arriving missionary. When a congregation calls a pastor here in North America, they look not only for the Master of Divinity, representing academic qualifications, but also for references as to godliness, integrity, and moral character. The church and the agency who send missionary candidates need to be equally as diligent in assessing those who will go cross-culturally.

Missionaries who know how to pray and who know the "power" of the Lord for effective ministry are needed more than ever. A.W. Tozer says of this power:

> It is not eloquence; it is not logic; it is not argument. It is not these things, though it may accompany any or all of them. It is more penetrating than thought, more disconcerting than conscience, more convincing than words. It is the subtle wonder that follows true Holy Spirit inspired preaching, a mysterious operation of spirit upon spirit. Such power must be present in some degree before anyone can be saved. It is the ultimate enabling without which the most earnest seeker must fall short of true saving faith.[6]

Many agencies have exciting histories of God's intervention in the lives of mission pioneers. Many of us marvel at the faith responses of Hudson Taylor, William Carey, and C.T. Studd. But each of these giants of mission history would argue that what is needed to meet present obstacles is the same expression of the extraordinary life of God in the faithful lives of ordinary men and women of this generation.

The need for the empowering life of God reaches beyond being able to preach a message which moves the hearts of hearers and extends to ability to work in true partnership with local leaders and co-workers— a perseverance in learning language and culture to the level that deep "heart" issues are understood and can be communicated.

Servant leadership is required, so that the missionary is genuinely content to not "call the shots" and manage the affairs of all but desires to enable and facilitate the ministry of others.

We reproduce spiritually *what we are.* Are we happy with the kind of Christians being formed in churches as a result of our missions activity? Increasingly there is a call for holistic discipleship in which Christians learn to love God with all their heart, mind, soul, and strength, and to love their neighbors in the area of marketplace ethics, integrity, and moral behavior. Are we as missionaries modeling this life in servant fashion?

The enabling for all of this accompanies understanding and increased spiritual devotion and intimacy. Keith Price, a minister-at-large with the Evangelical Fellowship of Canada, suggests the following regimen for the would-be missionary:

For 20 years I have encouraged the cultivation of the inner life. I now find myself, with equal fervor, mustering support for sustaining and strengthening crucial outreach initiatives and frontier missions. Never settle for just one or the other. . . .

a. Ask God for the ability to recognize imbalance in your life.

b. Nurture the inner life for all you are worth.

c. Encourage and be involved in productive mission projects.

d. Cut back without apology when activity approaches the frenetic.

e. Balance church growth and missionary talk with Bible reading and classics on the inner life.

f. Cultivate a deep hunger after God.

g. Be convinced that godliness, if genuine, will father social and evangelistic endeavors.

h. Make provision to spend time alone with God and keep it an essential. [7]

Price also has a warning for us:

In our increasingly "spirituality-interested" society, we must be conscious of the pendulum swing from frenetic religious activity on the one hand to settling down in the cloister and avoiding the world on the other. Some have been so lost in the wonder, love and praise of the contemplative life that the exciting momentum in foreign missions will slow to a snail's pace and the church-growth movement will be filed away into its narrow slot in history. [8]

The Holy Spirit's ministry and responsibility is to guide us into the right combination of contemplation, intimacy, and service. It is our responsibility to listen and obey. Richard Lovelace, Professor of Church History at Gordon-Conwell Seminary, reminds us of the message of Jonathan Edwards:

> Real Christianity requires encounter with truth, but that truth must be illuminated by the presence of the Holy Spirit. Only this can produce "a true sense of the divine excellency of the things revealed in the Word of God." One of the effects of this encounter will be a delight in the glory of God. The convert "does not merely rationally believe that God is glorious, but he has a sense of the gloriousness of God in his heart . . . there is a sense of the loveliness of God's holiness." Biblical Christianity is therefore a Spirit-illumined orthodoxy that transforms the heart and reorients the whole life to focus on God and seek his will. [9]

Though it may not hurt to stress the desperate needs of the world, the greater need in this day may be that Christians find a new satisfaction in a deeper intimacy with Jesus. Out of that intimacy will come listening hearts, who, when the Master asks "Who will go for Me?," will want to please Him and *go*.

In Closing

The decline in North American missionary numbers is not a harbinger of defeat. We repeat, God is not wringing His hands in frustration and anxiety over figures and statistics. The Lord of the universe is not bemoaning those who do not respond to the privilege of glorifying His Name among the nations. He will complete that which He has begun! "The transcendent message of God's sure triumph gives us the necessary distance and sobriety in respect to this world as well as the motivation to involve ourselves in the transformation of the status quo. Precisely the vision of God's triumph makes it impossible to look for sanctuary in quietism, neutrality, or withdrawal from the field of action." [10]

The "Baby Boomer" report by Engel and Jones makes clear that because of the present low priority given to world evangelization, recruiting strategies must change. Mission agencies must be aware of "paradigm shifts" with the onslaught of modernity and cultural change. Creative thinking in a biblical context is required, and a response which stimulates both the mentoring of "developing world" missions structures and encourages career missionary applications from North Americans is essential.

With all the discussion about paradigm changes (and there have been many positive, Spirit-inspired changes), one paradigm that certainly has not changed is what Jesus requires of those who would be His disciples: "If anyone would come after me, he must deny himself and take up his cross and follow me. For whoever wants to save his life will lose it, but whoever loses his life for me and for the gospel will save it" (Mark 8:34b–35).

The North American church has been invaded by the dependency movement prevalent in this culture and has encouraged Christians to increase self-esteem by loving themselves. The Scriptures warn us of days when "there will be terrible times," when "people will be lovers of themselves, lovers of money ... having a form of godliness but denying its power" (2 Timothy 3:1–5). May God visit the North American church yet again with authentic spiritual renewal as in the great historic revivals of the past. This always brings increased involvement in missions, and we could see "the knowledge of the glory of the Lord covering the earth as the waters cover the sea" within our generation.

Consider this comment from Herbert Kane in *Wanted: World Christians*:

> Of one thing we may be sure. The modern missionary movement is God's enterprise, not man's, and He is well able to take care of His own enterprise. The kingdom is His, the church is His, the power is His, and the glory is His. In spite of all evidence to the contrary, this world is God's world. He is in ultimate control, and He has no intention whatever of abdicating. The missionary movement of our time is part and parcel of His plan for the world, and it will continue to the end of the age. [11]

FOOTNOTES

INTRODUCTION

[1] Stan Guthrie, "New *Handbook* Reveals Drop in U.S. Missionaries," *World Pulse*, April 23, 1993, p. 1.

[2] James F. Engel and Jerry D. Jones, *Baby Boomers and the Future of World Missions* (Orange, Ca.: Management Development Associates, 1989), p. 20.

[3] Ibid., p. 22.

[4] James Reapsome, editorial, *World Pulse*, September 9, 1994, p. 4.

[5] Dr. James Dobson, *When God Doesn't Make Sense* (Wheaton: Tyndale House, ©1993), pp. 29-30.

CHAPTER ONE

[1] Engel, op. cit., p. 22.

[2] Doug Christgau, "Funding Missions: The Challenge of the '90s," *International Journal of Frontier Missions*, July-August 1994, p. 167.

[3] Doug LeBlanc, "New Budget Cuts Missions," *Christianity Today*, April 25, 1994, p. 26.

[4] Robert Coote, "Good News, Bad News: North American Protestant Overseas Personnel Statistics in Twenty-Five Year Perspective," *International Bulletin of Missionary Research*, January 1995, p. 6.

[5] Ibid., p. 7.

[6] Ibid., p. 8.

[7] John Siewert and John Kenyon, eds., 11th Edition *Mission Handbook* (Monrovia: MARC, 1993), p. 23.

[8] Ibid., p. 55.

[9] Engel, op. cit., p. 32.

CHAPTER TWO

[1] William Bennett, *Index of Cultural Indicators* (Washington, D.C., The Heritage Foundation, 1993), p. ii.

[2] Mark Hinton, "The Decline of American Culture," *Worldwide Thrust*, November-December 1993, p. 3.

[3] Daniel Yankelovich, *New Rules—Searching for Self-Fulfillment in a World Turned Upside Down* (New York: Random House, 1981), p. 33.

[4] George Barna and William Paul McKay, *Vital Signs: Emerging Social Trends and the Future of American Christianity* (Westchester, Ill.: Crossway Books, 1984), p. 4.

[5] Yankelovich, op. cit., pp. 98-99.

[6] Richard John Neuhaus, in Jonathan Alter and Pat Wingert's article, "The Return of Shame," *Newsweek*, February 6, 1995, p. 22.

[7] Leith Anderson, *Dying for Change* (Minneapolis: Bethany House, 1990), p. 84.

[8] Ibid., p. 35.

[9] Richard A. Gardner and Laura Mae Gardner, "Profiles of a Baby Boomer and Implications for Missions" (Unpublished paper, 1988), p. 11-12 (photocopied).

[10] George Barna, *Intervarsity*, Winter 1994, pp. 6-7.

[11] Bob Fryling, *Intervarsity*, Winter 1994, p. 5.

[12] Yankelovich, op. cit., pp. 242-246.

[13] Dr. Larry Crabb, Jr., *Finding God* (Grand Rapids: Zondervan Publishing House, 1993), p. 171.

[14] Leith Anderson, op. cit., p. 119.

[15] Crabb, op. cit., pp. 29-52.

[16] Barna, *Vital Signs*, p. 101.

[17] Cynthia Heald, "Experiencing God in the Day-to-Day," *Discipleship Journal*, January-February 1995, p. 60.

[18] David Bryant, *In the Gap*, p. 73. Another helpful study of World Christians is found in J. Herbert Kane's *Wanted: World Christians*, published by Baker Book House in 1986, with a particularly helpful description of "Why I believe in foreign missions."

[19] Donald G. Bloesch, *The Future of Evangelical Christianity* (New York: Doubleday and Co., 1983), p. 103.

[20] John Piper, *Let the Nations Be Glad. The Supremacy of God in Missions* (Grand Rapids: Baker Book House, 1993), p. 75.

²¹ Ibid., p. 110.

²² Mike Pollard, ed., *Cultivating a Missions-Active Church* (Wheaton: ACMC, 1988), p. 24.

²³ *The Pastor and Modern Missions: A Plea for Leadership in World Evangelization* (New York: Student Volunteer Movement for Foreign Missions, 1904).

²⁴ Ken Blue, *Healing Spiritual Abuse* (Downers Grove, Ill.: InterVarsity Press, 1993), p. 57. Other books on this subject include *The Subtle Power of Spiritual Abuse* by David Johnson and Jeff VanVonderan, *Churches That Abuse* by Ron Enroth, *Recovering from Spiritual Abuse* by Juanita and Dale Ryan, *Damaged Disciples* by Ron and Vicky Berk, *Toxic Faith* by Stephen Arterburn and Jack Felton, *Predators in Our Pulpits* by Philip Keller, *Productive Christians in an Age of Guilt Manipulation* by David Chilton, and *Letters to a Devastated Christian* by Gene Edwards.

²⁵ Andrew Murray, *The Ministry of Intercessory Prayer* (Minneapolis: Bethany House, 1981), pp. 57–59.

²⁶ David Rambo, "Death to Self, An Irreplaceable Truth," *Message of the Cross*, p. 11.

²⁷ C. S. Lewis, *Mere Christianity*, p. 12.

²⁸ Dwight Smith, in *Cultivating a Missions-Active Church* (Wheaton: ACMC, 1988), p. 12.

CHAPTER THREE

¹ David Blankenhorn, in Jonathan Alter's "The Name of the Game Is Shame," *Newsweek*, December 12, 1994, p. 41.

[2] Historically, the evangelical position on this subject has been to vigorously affirm the unending agony of those who die without Christ. There is a great deal of sound evangelical material on this subject. I personally found Millard Erickson's *Christian Theology* and John Piper's *Let the Nations Be Glad* helpful in deepening my understanding of the subject of annihilationism and its implications for missions. Other helpful texts include *Hell Is Under Fire* by Robert A. Peterson, *Crucial Questions About Hell* by Ajith Fernando, *The Other Side of the Good News* by Larry Dixon, *The Population of Heaven* by Ramesh Richard, *No Other Name: An Investigation Into the Destiny of the Unevangelized* by John Sanders, and *No Place for Truth, Or Whatever Happened to Evangelical Theology* by David F. Wells. Evangelical material supporting varying forms of annihilationism can be found in the recent writings of John Stott and Clark Pinnock.

[3] Clark Pinnock in Piper, op. cit., p. 116.

[4] David L. Edwards and John R.W. Stott, *Evangelical Essentials: A Liberal-Evangelical Dialogue* (IVP, Downers Grove: Ill., 1988), pp. 314-315.

[5] Anthony A. Hoekema, *The Bible and the Future* (Grand Rapids: Eerdmans Publishing, 1979), p. 273.

[6] Millard J. Erickson, *Christian Theology* (Grand Rapids: Baker Book House, 1985), p. 1240.

[7] Norman Anderson, ed., *The World's Religions: A Christian Approach to Comparative Religion* (Grand Rapids: Eerdmans, 1962), pp. 235-236.

[8] Millard J. Erickson, *Evangelical Missions Quarterly,* April 1975, p. 126.

⁹ February 1995 correspondence with Dr. Helen Roseveare.

¹⁰ William V. Crockett and James G. Sigountos, eds. "Are the Heathen Really Lost?" from *Through No Fault of Their Own?* (Grand Rapids: Baker Book House, 1991), p. 261.

CHAPTER FOUR

¹ Ruth Tucker, "Growing Up a World Away," *Christianity Today*, February 17, 1989.

² James Reapsome, "What's Holding Up World Evangelization? The Church Itself," *Evangelical Missions Quarterly*, April 1988, p. 119.

³ Laura Mae Gardner, "Parenting Problems Faced by Missionaries" (Wycliffe, 1977), p. 7 (photocopied).

⁴ Dan Harrison, "Causes and Effects of Changing Attitudes Toward Boarding Schools," *International Conference on Missionary Kids* (Manilla: Wycliffe, 1985), p. 302.

⁵ Raymond Chester, "To Send or Not to Send? Missionary Parents Ask," *Evangelical Missions Quarterly*, July 1984, pp. 252-259.

⁶ Ibid.

⁷ Ted Ward, "The Anxious Climate of Concern for Missionary Children," *International Bulletin of Missionary Research*, January 1989.

⁸ Ibid.

⁹ Ibid.

[10] Daniel Bacon, in *A Boy's War*, by David Michell (Singapore: OMF, 1988), p. iii.

[11] Ruth Tucker, "Growing Up a World Away," *Christianity Today*, February 17, 1989.

[12] Larry Sharp, "Boarding Schools—What Difference Do They Make?," *Evangelical Missions Quarterly*, January 1990, p. 26.

[13] Harrison, op. cit., p. 303.

CHAPTER FIVE

[1] Phil Parshall, "God's Communicator in the '90s," *Perspectives on the World Christian Movement*, edited by Ralph D. Winter and Steven C. Hawthorne (Pasadena: William Carey Library, 1992), p. C-31.

[2] Roger Greenway, "Eighteen Barrels and One Large Crate," *The Great Commission Handbook*, 1994, p. 26.

[3] Gardner, "Profiles of a Baby Boomer," op. cit., p. 4 (photocopied).

[4] Jonathan Bonk, *Mi$$ion$ and Money—Affluence as a Western Missionary Problem* (Maryknoll, N.Y.: Orbis Books, 1991), p. 45.

[5] Philip Slater, *The Pursuit of Loneliness: American Culture at the Breaking Point*, quoted in Bonk, p. 47.

[6] Bonk, op. cit., p. 42.

[7] Roland Allen, *Missionary Methods—St. Paul's or Ours?* (Grand Rapids: Eerdmans, 1962), pp. 49-60.

[8] A.W. Tozer, "The Blessedness of Possessing Nothing," in *Leadership*, edited by Paul D. Robbins, Spring 1981, p. 96.

[9] *World Pulse*, August 4, 1995, p. 3.

[10] Roberta Winter, *Mission Frontiers*, September-October 1994, pp. 23-24, 26-28.

[11] William Martin, *The Billy Graham Story—A Prophet with Honor* (London: Hutchinson Publishing, 1992), p. 124.

[12] John White, *The Golden Cow* (Downers Grove, Ill.: InterVarsity Press, 1979), pp. 102-103.

[13] Engel, op. cit., p. 53.

[14] Arthur T. Pierson, *George Müller of Bristol* (Old Tappan, N.J.: Fleming Revell Co., 1902.), p. 448.

[15] Roger Steer, *Delighted in God* (Singapore: OMF Publishing, 1985), p. 221.

[16] George and Donald Sweeting, *Lessons from the Life of Moody* (Chicago: Moody Press, 1989).

[17] Quoted from *Roots That Refresh* by Alister McGrath (London: Hodder and Stoughton, 1991).

CHAPTER SIX

[1] George Otis, "The Threshold Generation," *Charisma*, January 1995, p. 16.

[2] Michael Green, in *Planning Strategies for World Evangelization*, edited by Edward R. Dayton and David A. Fraser (Grand Rapids: Eerdmans, 1980), p. 196.

³ Ibid., p. 197.

⁴ G. Campbell Morgan, "The Revival: Its Source and Power," in *Glory Filled the Land: A Trilogy on the Welsh Revival*, edited by Richard Owen Roberts (Wheaton, Ill.: International Awakening Press, 1989), p. 174.

⁵ Jim Reapsome, "Robo Missionary: Multi-talented Savior," *World Pulse*, November 18, 1994, p. 4.

⁶ Allen, op. cit., pp. 156-157.

CHAPTER SEVEN

¹ Ralph Winter, "Money and Missions," *Mission Frontiers*, September-October 1994, p. 11.

² Ibid., p. 12.

³ Wade Coggins, "Can We Still Afford North American Missionaries?," *Mission Frontiers*, September-October 1994, p. 15.

⁴ Craig Ott, "Let the Buyer Beware," *Evangelical Missions Quarterly*, July 1993, pp. 286-291.

⁵ Wade Coggins, in Ott, ibid., p. 291.

⁶ K.P. Yohannan, *The Coming Revolution in World Missions* (Altamonte Springs: Creation House, 1986), pp. 142-147.

⁷ Larry Poston, "Should the West Stop Sending Missionaries?," *Evangelical Missions Quarterly*, January 1992, p. 61.

⁸ Ibid., p. 62.

[9] Robertson McQuilkin, "Six Inflammatory Questions, Part 1," *Evangelical Missions Quarterly*, April 1994, p. 134.

[10] Ibid., p. 134.

[11] Lawrence E. Keyes, "The New Age of Missions: A Study of Third World Missionary Societies," Doctoral Dissertation, Fuller Theological Seminary, p. 1 (photocopied).

[12] Luis Bush and Lorry Lutz, *Partnering in Ministry, The Direction of World Evangelism* (Downers Grove, Ill.: InterVarsity Press, 1990), p. 89.

[13] James Engel, "The Reengineering of World Missions," Unpublished article, 1994, p. 9 (photocopied).

[14] Ibid., p. 4.

[15] William Taylor in *World Pulse* article by Stan Guthrie, "Is the Grass Really Greener?," October 6, 1995, p. 2.

[16] Ruth Stoik Anaya, "Cross-Cultural Friendship—Doing Theology Globally" (Regent College, 1990), p. 18-19 (photocopied).

[17] Stan Guthrie, "Looking Under the Hood of the Non-Western Missions Movement," *Evangelical Missions Quarterly*, January 1995, p. 88.

[18] Ibid., p. 92.

[19] Phil Butler, President of Interdev, *EMQ*, October 1965, pp. 409-410.

CHAPTER EIGHT

[1] James F. Engel and Jerry D. Jones, op. cit., p. 23.

[2] STEM Ministries, "Is Short-Term Mission Really Worth the Time and Money—Results of Short-Term Mission Research" (Minneapolis: STEM, 1991), pp. 7-18.

[3] Ibid., p. 18.

[4] Coote, op. cit., p. 12.

[5] Robertson McQuilkin, "Six Inflammatory Questions, Part 2," *Evangelical Missions Quarterly*, July 1994, p. 260.

[6] Jim Reapsome, "The Peril of Drive-Thru Mission Work," *World Pulse*, June 25, 1993, p. 2.

[7] George Walker, "A Few Days' Sympathy" (Wewak, Papua New Guinea, photocopied).

CHAPTER NINE

[1] Don Hamilton, ed., *Tentmakers Speak: Practical Advice from Over 400 Missionary Tentmakers* (Duarte, Ca.: TMQ Research, 1987), p. 9.

[2] Jim Reapsome, ed., *World Pulse*, November 4, 1994, p. 5.

[3] Robertson McQuilkin, *EMQ*, July 94, p. 261.

CHAPTER TEN

[1] U.S. Center for World Mission, "The Hope and Challenge of World Evangelization," September 1, 1992, p. 1 (photocopied).

[2] Bloesch, op. cit., p. 126.

[3] F.B. Meyer, message entitled, "Preparation for Christian Service," *Student Volunteer Movement for Foreign Missions. The Student Missionary Appeal*, p. 10.

[4] Ralph Winter, "Countdown 2000 to World Evangelization" (Pasadena: U.S. Center for World Mission), p. 15 (photocopied).

[5] Luis Bush, "The Changing Role of the U.S. Church in World Evangelism," *Missions Today '94*, p. 10.

[6] Patrick Johnstone, *News Circular-WEC International Research Office*, January 9, 1995, p. 1 (photocopied).

[7] Ibid., p. 2

CHAPTER ELEVEN

[1] Andres Tapia, "Reaching the First Post-Christian Generation," quoting William Mahedy and Janet Bernardi, *A Generation Alone: Xers Making a Place in the World*; in *Christianity Today*, September 12, 1994.

[2] Ron Luce, "How Can We Reach Generation X?," *Charisma*, September 1994, p. 20-27.

[3] Evelyn Hibbert, "Bulgaria: Miracle Among the Millet," *World Pulse*, November 3, 1995, p. 4.

[4] Eric Thurman, "Empty Bellies Don't Have Ears," *Missions Today '95*, p. 36.

[5] William Taylor, "Lessons in Partnership," *EMQ*, October 1995, p. 411.

[6] A.W. Tozer editorial, *The Alliance Weekly*, date unknown.

[7] Keith Price, "From Cloisterphobia to Cloister-mania," *Faith Today*, January-February 1994, p. 41.

[8] Ibid.

[9] Richard Lovelace, "The Surprising Works of God," *Christianity Today*, September 11, 1995, p. 28.

[10] David J. Bosch, *Transforming Mission: Paradigm Shifts in Theology of Mission* (Maryknoll, N.Y.: Orbis Books, 1991), p. 510.

[11] Herbert J. Kane, *Wanted: World Christians*, (Grand Rapids: Baker Book House, 1986), p. 132.

BIBLIOGRAPHY

ACMC. *Your Church: Designing a Missions Strategy & Your Church: Stimulating Missions Involvement.* Wheaton: ACMC, 1990.

ACMC. *Cultivating a Missions-Active Church.* Wheaton: ACMC, 1988.

Allen, Roland. *Missionary Methods, St. Paul's or Ours?* Grand Rapids: Eerdmans, 1962.

Allen, Roland. *Spontaneous Expansion of the Church.* Grand Rapids: Eerdmans, 1962.

Alter, Jonathan. "The Name of the Game Is Shame." *Newsweek,* Dec. 12, 1994, p. 41.

Anaya, Ruth Stoik. "Cross-Cultural Friendship—Doing Theology Globally." Vancouver, B.C.: Unpublished paper presented to Regent College faculty, Dec. 3, 1990 (photocopy).

Anderson, Leith. *Dying for Change.* Minneapolis: Bethany Publishers, 1990.

Anderson, Norman, ed. *The World's Religions: A Christian Approach to Comparative Religion.* Grand Rapids: Eerdmans, 1962.

Barna, George and William Paul McKay. *Vital Signs: Emerging Social Trends and the Future of American Christianity.* Westchester, Ill.: Crossway Books, 1984.

Bennett, William J. *Index of Leading Cultural Indicators*. Washington, D.C.: The Heritage Foundation, 1993.

Berry, Bill, publisher of *Missions Today '94* magazine. Evanston, Ill.: Berry Publishing. 1994.

Bloesch, Donald G. *The Future of Evangelical Christianity*. New York: Doubleday and Co., 1983.

Blue, Ken. *Healing Spiritual Abuse*. Downers Grove, Ill.: InterVarsity Press, 1993.

Bonk, Jonathan. *Mi$$ion$ and Money—Affluence as a Western Missionary Problem*. Maryknoll, N.Y.: Orbis Books, 1991.

Borthwick, Paul. *A Mind for Missions: Ten Ways to Build Your World Vision*. Colorado Springs: NavPress, 1990.

Bosch, David J. *Transforming Mission: Paradigm Shifts in Theology of Mission*. Maryknoll, N.Y.: Orbis Books, 1991.

Bryant, David. *In the Gap*. Madison, Wis.: InterVarsity Fellowship, 1979.

Bush, Luis. "The Changing Role of the U.S. Church in World Evangelism." *Missions Today '94*. Evanston, Ill.: Berry Publishing, 1994, pp. 8-10.

Bush, Luis and Lorry Lutz. *Partnering in Ministry, The Direction of World Evangelism*. Downers Grove, Ill.: InterVarsity Press, 1990.

Christgau, Doug. "Funding Missions: The Challenge of the '90s." *International Journal of Frontier Missions*. July-Aug. 1994, p. 167.

Coggins, Wade. "Can We Still Afford North American Missionaries?" *Mission Frontiers*, Sept.-Oct. 1994, pp. 14-15.

Coote, Robert T. "Good News, Bad News: North American Protestant Overseas Personnel Statistics in Twenty-Five Year Perspective." *International Bulletin of Missionary Research*. New Haven, Ct.: Overseas Ministries Study Center, Jan. 1995, pp. 6-12.

Crabb Jr., Dr. Larry. *Finding God*. Grand Rapids: Zondervan Publishing House, 1993.

Crockett, William V. and James G. Sigountos, eds. *Through No Fault of Their Own?* Grand Rapids: Baker Book House, 1991.

Current Thoughts and Trends. Vol. 10, No. 11, November, 1994. Colorado Springs: Navigators, 1994.

Dayton, Edward R. and David A. Fraser, *Planning Strategies for World Evangelization*. Grand Rapids: Eerdmans, 1980.

Dobson, Dr. James. *When God Doesn't Make Sense*. Wheaton: Tyndale House, ©1993.

Engel, James F. and Jerry D. Jones. *Baby Boomers & the Future of World Missions*. Orange, Ca.: Management Development Associates, 1989.

Engel, James F. and Wilbert Norton. *What's Gone Wrong with the Harvest?* Grand Rapids: Academie Books, 1975.

Engel, James F. "The Reengineering of World Missions." St. Davids, Pa.: Unpublished paper from Eastern College, 1994 (photocopy).

Erickson, Millard J. *Christian Theology.* Grand Rapids: Baker Book House, 1985.

Gardner, Richard A. and Laura Mae Gardner. "Profiles of a Baby Boomer and Implications for Missions." Unpublished paper, 1988 (photocopy).

Global Mapping International Newsletter. Global Mapping Project. Fall-Winter 1994, p. 2.

Guthrie, Stan. "New *Handbook* Reveals Drop in U.S. Missionaries." *World Pulse,* April 23, 1993, pp. 1-2.

Hamilton, Don, ed. *Tentmakers Speak: Practical Advice from Over 400 Missionary Tentmakers.* Duarte, Ca.: TMQ Research, 1987.

Heald, Cynthia. "Experiencing God in the Day-to-Day." *Discipleship Journal,* Jan.-Feb. 1995, p. 60.

Hesselgrave, David. *Today's Choices For Tomorrow's Mission: An Evangelical Perspective on Trends and Issues in Missions.* Grand Rapids: Zondervan, 1988.

Hibbert, Evelyn. "Bulgaria: Miracle Among the Millet." *World Pulse,* Nov. 3, 1995, p. 4.

Hinton, Mark. "The Decline of American Culture." *Worldwide Thrust,* Nov.-Dec. 1993, pp. 3-5.

Hoekema, Anthony A. *The Bible and the Future.* Grand Rapids: Eerdmans, 1979.

Hunter, James. *Evangelicalism in the Coming Generation.* Chicago, Ill.: University of Chicago Press, 1987.

Johnstone, Patrick. *Operation World.* Grand Rapids: Zondervan, 1993.

Kane, Herbert J. *Wanted: World Christians.* Grand Rapids: Baker Book House, 1986.

Kunde, Neil. *Intervarsity Magazine*. Madison, Wis.: Inter-Varsity Christian Fellowship. Winter 1994.

Le Blanc, Doug. "New Budget Cuts Missions." *Christianity Today*, April 25, 1994, p. 47.

Lewis, Jonathan, ed. *Working Your Way to the Nations: A Guide to Effective Tentmaking*. Pasadena: William Carey Library, 1993.

Martin, William. *The Billy Graham Story—A Prophet with Honor*. London: Hutchinson Publishing, 1992.

McCoy, Gary D. "The Shrinking Missionary Force." *Moody Monthly*, Fall 1993, pp. 6-10.

McQuilkin, Robertson. *The Great Omission*. Grand Rapids: Baker Book House, 1984.

McQuilkin, Robertson. "Six Inflammatory Questions, Part 1." *Evangelical Missions Quarterly*, April 1994, p. 134.

McQuilkin, Robertson. "Six Inflammatory Questions, Part 2." *Evangelical Missions Quarterly*, July 1994, p. 260-261.

Michell, David. *A Boy's War*. Singapore: Overseas Missionary Fellowship Publishing, 1988.

Murray, Andrew. *The Ministry of Intercessory Prayer*. Minneapolis: Bethany House, 1981.

Ott, Craig. "Let the Buyer Beware." *Evangelical Missions Quarterly*, July 1993, pp. 286-293.

Pierson, Arthur T. *George Müller of Bristol*. Old Tappan, New Jersey: Fleming Revell Co., 1902.

Piper, John. *Let the Nations Be Glad. The Supremacy of God in Missions*. Grand Rapids: Baker Book House, 1993.

Rambo, David. "Death to Self, An Irreplaceable Truth." *Message of the Cross.* Minneapolis: Bethany Publishers, Oct.-Dec. 1994.

Raymo, Judy. *Family and Ministry?* Unpublished paper, 1992 (photocopy).

Reapsome, James. "The Peril of Drive-Thru Mission Work." *World Pulse,* June 25, 1993, p. 2.

Reapsome, James. "Robo Missionary: Multi-talented Savior." *World Pulse,* Nov. 18, 1994, p. 4.

Reapsome, James W., ed. *Evangelical Missions Quarterly,* April, 1975; Jan. 1992; Jan. 1995.

Rieff, Philip. *The Triumph of the Therapeutic.* New York: Harper and Row, 1966.

Siewert, John A. and John Kenyon, eds. *Mission Handbook.* Monrovia, Ca.: MARC, a division of World Vision International, 1993.

Steer, Roger. *Delighted in God.* Singapore: OMF Publishing, 1985.

Steer, Roger. *J. Hudson Taylor, A Man in Christ.* Singapore: OMF Publishing, 1990.

STEM Ministries. *Is Short-Term Mission Really Worth the Time and Money?—Results of STEM Short-Term Mission Research.* Minneapolis: STEM Ministries Inc., 1991.

Student Volunteer Movement for Foreign Missions. *The Student Missionary Appeal.* (Addresses at the Third International Convention of the SVMFM). New York: SVMFM, 1898. The *Pastor and Modern Missions: A Plea for Leadership in World Evangelization.* New York: SVMFM, 1904.

Sweeting, George and Donald. *Lessons from the Life of Moody.* Chicago: Moody Press, 1989.

Turabian, Kate L. *A Manual for Writers.* Chicago: University of Chicago Press, 1971.

White, John. *The Golden Cow.* Downers Grove Ill.: InterVarsity Press, 1979.

Wilson, J. Christy, Jr. *Today's Tentmakers.* Wheaton: Tyndale House, 1979.

Winter, Ralph D., ed. "Money and Missions." *Mission Frontiers,* Sept.-Oct. 1994, pp. 10-13, 23-24, 26-28.

Winter, Ralph D. and Steven C. Hawthorne. *Perspectives on the World Christian Movement.* Pasadena: William Carey Library, 1992.

Woodward, Kenneth L. "Whatever Happened to Sin?" *Newsweek,* Feb. 6, 1995, p. 23.

Yankelovich, Daniel. *New Rules—Searching for Self-Fulfillment in a World Turned Upside Down.* New York: Random House, 1981.

Yohannan, K.P. *The Coming Revolution in World Missions.* Altamonte Springs, Fl.: Creation House, 1986.

My address and phone number are:

Jim Raymo
P.O. Box 1707
Fort Washington, Pa. 19034
(215) 646-2322

*   *   *   *   *

This book was produced by the Christian Literature Crusade. We hope it has been helpful to you in living the Christian life. CLC is a literature mission with ministry in over 45 countries worldwide. If you would like to know more about us, or are interested in opportunities to serve with a faith mission, we invite you to write to:

Christian Literature Crusade
P.O. Box 1449
Fort Washington, PA 19034